HEATHER RUTISHAUSER

BREAK FREE

How Following the Signs
Led Me to Myself

Cover Art by Tania Radermacher — tanias.socials@gmail.com
Headshot Photography by Gabor Kozmon — @gaborkozmon

ISBN: 979-8-9923383-0-0 (printed edition)
ISBN: 979-8-9923383-1-7 (eBook edition)

Published by Meehan & Thayer Press

For more information visit **www.athenarosealchemy.com**

EXPERIENCE THE MAGIC

This book is full of wild coincidences, strange encounters, and moments that seem too good to be true. But all of it really happened. I *lived* it.

You don't have to take my word for it, because I made sure to document the magic along the way! I've created a digital scrapbook so you can experience the story firsthand. Follow along chapter by chapter and watch the moments unfold in real time!

—heather ♥

Scan the QR code below or go to **www.athenarosealchemy.com/ break-free-bonuses** for free access to the *Break Free Scrapbook*, a meditation guide, and other additional resources!

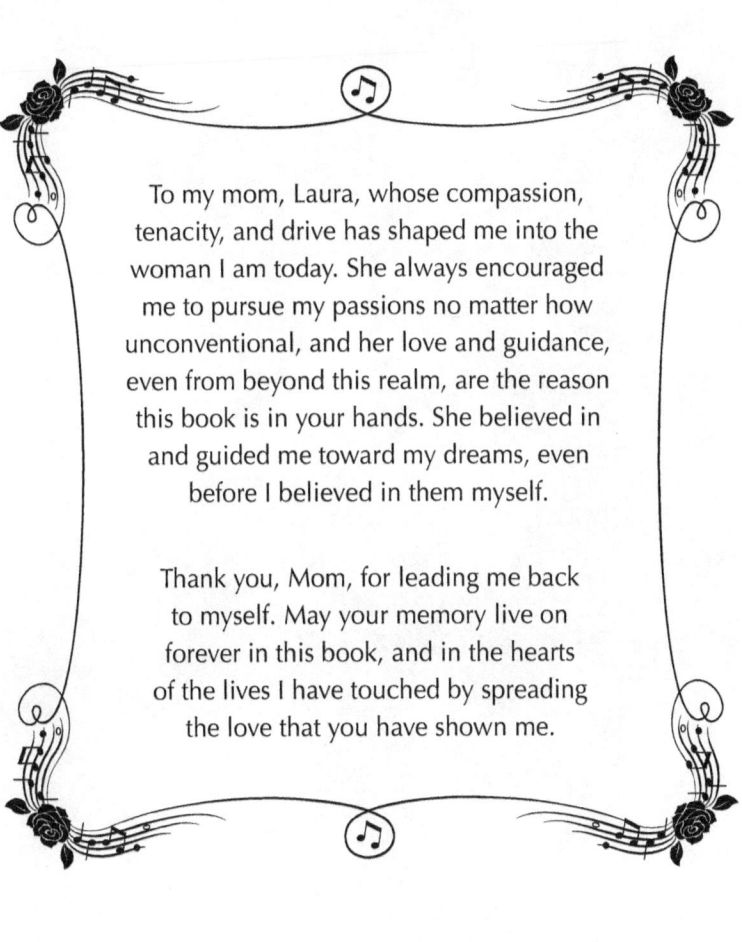

To my mom, Laura, whose compassion, tenacity, and drive has shaped me into the woman I am today. She always encouraged me to pursue my passions no matter how unconventional, and her love and guidance, even from beyond this realm, are the reason this book is in your hands. She believed in and guided me toward my dreams, even before I believed in them myself.

Thank you, Mom, for leading me back to myself. May your memory live on forever in this book, and in the hearts of the lives I have touched by spreading the love that you have shown me.

Stories are medicine … They have
such power; they do not require that
we do, be, act anything—
we need only listen.
—Clarissa Pinkola Estés, *Women Who
Run with the Wolves*

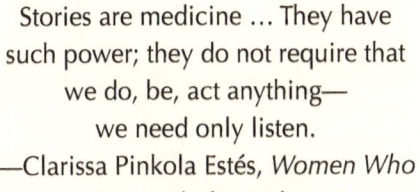

AUTHOR'S NOTE

Every few weeks she would shut herself up in
her room, put on her scribbling suit, and
'fall into a vortex', as she expressed it,
writing away at her novel with all her
heart and soul, for till that was finished
she could find no peace.
—Louisa May Alcott, *Little Women*

I've rewritten this introduction a thousand times—it's hard to find any words. What do you say when standing on the doorstep of your biggest dream? What do you say when something you've imagined for your entire life is now about to become a reality?

For as long as I can remember, books have been my safe space. I grew up in a world that was endlessly confusing to me, and I was never quite sure how I would fit into it. In fact, I didn't believe that I ever would. I figured I was a bug in the system. There must have been some mistake made up in the cosmos when they decided to send *me* down to earth.

While the real world was an awful and confusing place, books had always welcomed me with open arms. Paper and ink wrapped themselves around me in a warm embrace. Over the years, as I left the library countless times with my stacks of solace, I dreamed of one day seeing my name written across one of the fancy covers.

There was only one problem: I had always had difficulty telling anything but the truth. So fiction was a no-go.

And my *real* life? Well, there was nothing special about *that*. But a girl can dream.

Now I know there is power in dreaming.

You see, in the summer of 2023, I watched with wonder as my life—*my actual, real-world life*—turned to magic in front of my eyes. I saw myself reflected in the characters I had read about for so long, and the chapters of my story unfolded perfectly before me. So perfectly, in fact, it seemed as if the plot had already been penned down weeks before by some ambitious writer hiding behind a screen. The second something significant would occur, a smile would spread across my face. *This is the next chapter!* I would think to myself. I began writing this book before I even knew how it would end, because I was still *living* it. And I think the most powerful stories are written that way. The unknown is where the magic dwells, waiting to rise within us.

It's funny that I mention magic, because the girl you'll meet on the very next page thought that magic was reserved *only* for her fiction books.

In May of 2023, where our story really kicks off, I was just an ordinary twenty-three-year-old. I had major self-esteem and confidence issues. I was a people pleaser. I had social anxiety. I was afraid to speak my mind or be seen by others. I was drowning in grief. I was living in San Diego, California, and working as a photojournalist in the toxic world of news while rapidly approaching severe burnout. I also didn't believe in any higher power, had no idea why I was on this earth, and had no clue how I was going to survive on it for another sixty years of my life, let alone the next five.

That girl might have been called Heather, but only in name. That girl was not *me*.

As I write this introduction a year and a half later, I am a spiritual and authenticity mentor with an online community of eighty thousand people and growing. I communicate with my spirit guides and the universe regularly and teach people how they can do the same. I guide others on how to live free from the fears and constraints that keep them trapped within their minds, and speak my truth with a confidence and a presence I never knew I had within me. Also, I've been living nomadically abroad for an entire *year*.

I am genuinely happy about my life and where I am going, and I have never felt more sure of who I am and what I am capable of. I know that this book is *only the beginning*.

So how did I get here?

It's a question I've been asked by numerous people. And it's a question that is impossible to answer in a few sentences. In fact, to even attempt such a simplification would diminish the profound transformation I underwent. So instead, I am providing my answer here in this book.

This past year, I have told a few people in passing that I am publishing a memoir. "A memoir?" they all ask, the shock evident on their faces. "How old are you?"

"Twenty-four", I reply—my next birthday passed while the manuscript was still in the editing phase.

"Twenty-four?" they say, "And a memoir? But you're so very *young*. What story would *you* have to tell?"

I just smile to myself. And sometimes a few tears spring into my eyes.

Because it's exactly this type of "realist" and "typical" thinking that kept me a pawn on the chess board all my life, afraid to make any moves. Afraid that I wasn't old *enough*, or experienced *enough*, or capable *enough*, or smart *enough*, or professional *enough*, or a million and one other *enoughs* that my brain conjured out of the dark every second of the day to imprison me.

You'll never be enough, it said.

I'll tell you right now that *you are enough for anything that you want to do in this life*. All you need is the courage to go out and reach for it with *everything* you have, and the discernment to know that *almost everyone* you know will try to instill doubt in you.

There's a quote by George Moore that I love, "Reality can destroy the dream; why shouldn't the dream destroy reality?"

Don't trust people who spend their precious time telling other people how to use theirs. Most people in this world—whether they realize it or not—carry around a sledgehammer, using "realism" as a guise to smash dreams into pieces.

Well I carry around a different hammer. I enjoy smashing *reality* to bits whenever I can.

This book is for the dreamers, the ones who spend their days with their nose in a book, and wrapped in whimsy rather than a suit jacket. It's for the outcasts, who knew the way they wanted to live but never saw it modeled by anyone around them. It's for the people who follow what everyone else is doing, but feel it in their bones that they're meant for more. And it's for the girls who felt like they had to spend their whole life hiding who they truly were, for approval, for connection, for love.

I spent my whole life trying to look for a place where I felt safe, where I felt like I truly belonged. I've now realized that *I* am the one who is supposed to create that place.

So here it is. This is the book that I wish I had as I grew up—when I felt lost, alone, and unsure of where to turn to for answers.

To understand how I got to where I am today, we must dive deep into some painful memories. Because *everything* I know now, I have only learned because I had experienced the direct opposite, and I decided I didn't like the way it feels. I decided there had to be a different path.

And if there wasn't, *I would make one.*

So I did. I got out my shovel and started digging. Into the past, into the pain, and into every identity I had clung onto to make sense of who I was. And what I found was more peace, contentment, and fulfillment than most people experience in their entire lifetimes. And I'm only twenty-four.

But we can do better than that. I want the teenagers and young twenty-somethings to read this book now and enact their own changes to find fulfillment and peace, without knowing the struggle and pain that this book is born out of. Without waking up in their thirties, forties, or fifties, looking back at the decades they put into a career, and regretting that they never really *lived*.

This is my story, but for you, it is a mirror. A mirror to lead you back to yourself. The answers are waiting for you, if only you have the courage to find them.

I'm used to being an open book, but becoming an open *published* book is definitely new territory. I've always said that I express myself in writing in ways that I can't when I speak, which means this book is both my source of liberation, and a deep act of vulnerability. Thank you so much for your time and your trust with my story as you venture on to the next pages.

I WROTE A BOOK!!!!!!!!! You are holding my dream in your hands. It is my hope that it will inspire you to go out and create your own, whatever that may be. Welcome to the magic :)

—heather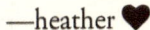

TABLE OF CONTENTS

PROLOGUE

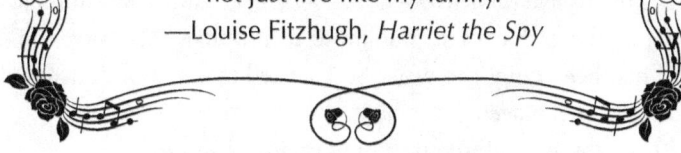

There is as many ways to live as there are
people on the earth and I shouldn't go round
with blinders but should see every way I can.
Then I'll know what way I want to live and
not just live like my family.
—Louise Fitzhugh, *Harriet the Spy*

When I was young, I lived my life in fiction. Magic and dragons, murderous plots and sorcerer's stones. It was easier to tolerate than the real world I found myself hopelessly stuck in.

I read *Harriet the Spy* over and over again in elementary school. I was especially drawn to that book. Illustrated on the cover was a potted plant with a girl crouching behind it, writing in a composition notebook. Little eleven-year-old Harriet, the aspiring spy and writer.

I liked to imagine it was me on the cover, behind that plant.

Heather the Spy.

I hoped my observations would earn me a book someday.

I clutched my 99-cent composition notebook—the kind with the black and white marble cover—close to my chest everywhere I went. I would sit and write about the people I saw around me. Just making observations. Just trying to make sense of this confusing world I was brought into.

When I was young, I asked a lot of questions. This was before I learned you're not supposed to do that. Adults don't like questions.

They call it talking back.

"You'll understand when you're older."

That was the age-old response to my inquiries. I waited and waited for the day that everything would finally make sense. But a decade later, suddenly an "adult" myself, I understood even less than I did back in elementary school, sitting on the slide with my little notebook.

In fact, now that I'm older, I look up, and everyone around me—family, coworkers, the "successful" business leaders we're taught to admire, people who claim to have it "all figured out," who tell others how to live their lives—looks *miserable*. And *I* was miserable. I *had* to believe that there was more to life than the conventional path I had been taught to walk. So I started to search for answers in unconventional places.

This book is a culmination of what I have found.

AFTER

That's the mystery, isn't it? Is the labyrinth living or dying? Which is he trying to escape—the world or the end of it?
—John Green, *Looking for Alaska*

Get off the elevator. Take a right. Then a left. Walk straight and through the sliding glass doors. Enter the Neuro ICU.

If I close my eyes, I can still see the exact hallway layout of Westchester Medical Center in Valhalla, New York.

There was a quiet, but tangible pain as I walked the steps and realized that this path was becoming familiar. I could feel the turns cementing along my neural pathways.

The hospital was becoming my new normal.

The brain surgery had gone well, but Mom was still in a coma. "Just waiting to see when she wakes up," they said.

Her room was at the very end of the ICU unit. There were printed out family photos taped to the wall beyond the sliding glass doors. Across from them, the stuffed Build-A-Bear bunny I got my mom for Mother's Day that year, was lying on the corner of the bed. *Best Mom Ever*, read its small pink tee.

And there was Mom, lying there, next to that bunny, though it didn't really *feel* like Mom. Her face was shrunken, her limbs swollen, and part of her curly brown hair was shaved off from her head.

To me, Mom was always warmth, light, and love. In this room I only ever felt cold, lost, and disconnected.

I sometimes wonder if it would have been better if she had passed away that very first night after her stroke, rather than be stuck in this horrible in between. Some people might say that her three weeks in a coma provided us the opportunity to say goodbye, to prepare. But what it really did was give us hope. Hope that turned to dead weight in my chest on the night it all ended.

Speaking to Mom in that comatose state did not provide me with much closure. It was too cold in there. It just reminded me that her warmth was gone.

And it reeked of antiseptic.

Three weeks into college, and suddenly I had become *The Girl Whose Mom Just Died.*

I had to FaceTime my roommate and ask her to mail my black dress home to New York for the funeral. I'd known the girl for less than a month.

I mastered the art of crying silently in the middle of the night so as not to bother her. When it became too hard, I would go outside and sob in the hallway, watching the picture slideshow I had made for Mom's wake on a loop, hoping and praying that no one came out of their room to use the communal bathroom.

I wiped away the strings of brown hair stuck to my face and blinked through blurry eyes at the smiles on my computer screen. It was hard to watch, to see all those happy memories. That was my Before. Now I was stuck in the After, desperately trying to grasp onto something that I would never have again.

After.

That's what life felt like to me. My mom had her stroke on *the day* I moved into college. My life was neatly, perfectly divided into a Before and an After—the scissors of the Fates snipping my old life so clean off it resembled a storybook plot.

My brain loved to add subtitles too. Before, *when I was happy*, and After, *where I was now eternally miserable*.

I was cast off into the air without anything to anchor me, floating further and further away from who I was. A balloon shouldn't be tied down to too many things, but without at least one paperweight to secure it, it will drift into the atmosphere to its eventual demise.

Mom had been my rock.

The only way to make it back to the ground might be to carry my own anchor. But that sounded incredibly lonely. I felt like if I tried to carry any more weight, I might break.

My entire college experience was terrible. I was going through a life-shattering loss, surrounded by drunk, partying college kids I had only just met on our rural Connecticut campus. But I needed friends—I needed *someone*—so I did what everyone else was doing. I went to frat parties and drank myself into a stupor, inevitably falling apart as soon as I got back to my dorm.

Sometimes I didn't even make it back to the dorm. I have a few blurry memories of falling to the ground in random driveways in front of pledges, staring at the curves of a red solo cup until I could no longer see the reality I was living in. The girls I had come with—girls I had only *just* met—would try to help me get back home safely.

If I was fortunate enough to feign happiness and hold it in until I made it back to my floor, I would find corners of the hallway or the common room to cry in. I used to wrap my hands around my knees and bring them to my chest, willing myself to disappear. At the same time, I hoped that someone would find me and save me from myself.

A hopeless paradox.

I made some friends during college, but none of them stuck.

I'm not surprised, though. My grief probably made me difficult to be around. I could be a ray of light one minute, and completely withdrawn the next. I was on the sideline of every group I entered.

The pain was too much, so I continued to numb myself in every way possible. Drinking, smoking weed, binge eating, binge watching TV, doom scrolling on social media. I was terrified of being alone with my mind, so I did anything and everything to escape my thoughts.

It felt like I was in a completely different dimension from everyone else. I would sit with a group of girls at the campus dining hall. As everyone else ate and laughed and then casually mentioned their parents, I would sit silently, staring at the glinting silver tines of my fork until my mind floated off into a void.

I spent a lot of time in this void. I would look into mirrors and not recognize the eyes staring back. My consciousness lived in the air, and someone else was in my body.

I had expected these to be the best years of my life. God knows I had heard that enough. *Have fun at college, you will always wish you had this time back.*

I remember thinking to myself, *If these are my best years, then I don't want to be here anymore.* Sometimes I would dream of the reprieve of just going to sleep at night and never waking up.

When those thoughts got too loud, I would quiet them by thinking of my sisters. They would not be able to deal with another loss. It would hurt them too much if I was gone.

I was not even living for me anymore.

In the Wind

I am the daughter of a tall, strong tree. My
timber forms a ship, but it is anchorless,
flagless … if in doubt, always endure alone.
—Nina George, *The Little Paris Bookshop*

I had been hanging on by a thread while in college for a long time, but buying a FitBit at the beginning of 2020 is what finally pushed me to my breaking point. Ironically, this was only a week or two before the world hit its own breaking point.

You see, back in 2018, my mom was fine until she wasn't. She was fine until she came home from the doctor one day, telling us that she had a heart condition and needed surgery. Then she was fine until a few months later, when the doctor told her she had an infection. Then she was fine again until a few hours after she dropped me off at college my first year. One moment I was walking to the school's opening ceremony, and the next I was answering a call from my older sister, telling me that Mom had a stroke while on the drive home from campus.

She died three weeks later.

Nothing in my life felt safe anymore. *I* no longer felt safe anymore. I couldn't trust anything; I couldn't trust Mom's health, so I couldn't trust my own.

It was now my sophomore year, and the layer of snow on the ground was slowly giving way to patches of green. I walked the campus paths as the pit of dread in my stomach grew larger and larger by the day. I glanced down at the FitBit on my wrist while my breath caught in my throat—what had started as an innocent quest to track my habits and live a healthier lifestyle, had turned into an obsession. I found myself constantly checking my heart rate after stairs and exercises. My heart rate seemed higher than normal, and it didn't seem to come down as fast as it should. I was desperate to discover what was wrong with me.

At the end of February, I got the flu—this only made my stamina worse. My knuckles turned white as I gripped onto the railing and struggled with labored breath to make it up the three flights of stairs to my dorm room. Dealing with illness did anything but help my anxiety. I began to spiral into hysteria. A week before my spring break of 2020 began, my aunt (my mother's sister) and uncle came to pick me up from college so I could have some extra time to recover. None of us were expecting what came next.

A lot of things at once.

Apparently, my internal world wasn't the only thing going up in flames. I had gone home to try and heal from my health-based anxiety, but COVID-19 coming to New York did the exact opposite. I started living in fear every single day. I was already shattered by my mom's loss, and I knew I would not be able to handle it if another person I cared about was taken from my life. It felt like everything and everyone I loved was teetering dangerously close to the edge of a cliff. Being surrounded by so much talk of death a year and half after losing my mom was a lot to take.

At the same time …

Right after making it to my aunt and uncle's house, my dad dropped a bomb of his own. He was going to be selling our house—the house that I had lived in my entire life—and moving in with his new fiancé. We needed to have all our stuff out of the house by August.

Up until this point, I had always gone back *home* during college breaks—although with only my dad and I in the house, the silence was palpable. With my mental health going the way that it was, my aunt and uncle had thought it would be better for me to spend the spring break at their house this time. But that's *all* it was supposed to be. *Spring break.* Now suddenly I was moving my things into their guest room, "quarantine" was becoming a regular word in my vocabulary, and I had unknowingly lived my last days in my childhood home.

What the fuck is going on?

I don't want to blame my dad for his decision. This situation was rife with nuance and complex feelings. I used to think that the world was all black and white, but now I look around and all I see are endless shades of gray.

I could see my dad's reality so clearly in my mind's eye. Him with my mom dropping me off at college, beginning their drive home—*brand new empty nesters!* Then suddenly, she's *gone.* He returns to our house—the house they had lived in as a family for *twenty years*—and he's all alone. Everything about his life became completely different with no warning.

His After had begun too.

So I understand. I understand wanting to look for another person and not go through life alone. I understand the relief that must have come from finding someone to provide a new start, separate from all the pain. It made no sense to have one person living in that house all alone. At the same time, it hurt that he was making a choice to move on. He was moving away from the pain of the past, but it felt like he was moving away from *me*.

I didn't have the "new start" option. College was supposed to be my new start—my new home—and now I was getting an email announcement about a fully online spring semester. I looked away for *one second*, and now my campus was gone, *and* my childhood home was gone too. Everything was falling away from me *again*, and I had *no control* over it.

I settled into living in quarantine with my aunt and uncle at their home in upstate New York. I was grateful that they opened their home to me even as the timeline for my stay got drastically extended. I tried to adjust by making their guest room my new safe space, while simultaneously living in constant fear that something would happen to them and that sense of safety would be taken away from me too. I spent many of my days FaceTiming my two older sisters. One was a medical student living in New York City—the epicenter of the pandemic. The other was in Massachusetts, working in outpatient pediatrics. Both had a much higher risk of exposure working in medical settings.

I tried to remind myself that they were young and healthy, and likely nothing would happen to them. But nothing felt guaranteed anymore. Nowhere felt safe.

The next three months were spent finishing my semester online, trying not to think about any of my loved ones dying, driving to and from my childhood home to pick up boxes, renting a storage container in my aunt's driveway to sort through childhood memorabilia and Mom's old things, scheduling donation pickups, and crying. So much crying.

There was also something else.

My aunt, uncle, and I were all getting used to living together for the very first time, during a time when it seemed collectively like the *world* was ending. It was a very stressful and emotional situation, and we were all trying to cope with it in our own ways. Sometimes, these ways clashed.

Usually when this happened, it was without warning. I would think that things were fine, and then they weren't. There would be yelling. I had done something wrong, or broken an unspoken rule, or upset them in some way.

I noticed something strange as this started happening—the yelling felt *familiar* to me. The sense of dread and pit in my stomach when the tone or demeanor of someone in the house changed, felt familiar. The instant tense of my shoulders when I heard a footstep that sounded just a *little* too heavy to be indicative of a positive mood, felt familiar. Bracing myself before going downstairs, unaware of what situation I would walk into, felt familiar. And when I sat in that familiar feeling, I was no longer a twenty-year-old girl—I felt like I was a child.

It was the first time I realized that my childhood in the Before might not have been *all* sunshine and rainbows. It was the first time I realized that growing up in a household that was good a lot of the time, but also had a fair amount of unpredictable verbal and emotional conflict, had trained me to live in fear of tripping an unseen wire.

Again, a situation that was painted in shades of gray. There were so many ways in which I had a great and privileged childhood, and I am truly grateful for all my parents did for me.

But no one's home life is perfect. In fact, ignoring that truth is what keeps families at a distance, feigning perfection and keeping emotions bottled up over time. Naming things is a powerful tool, one that allows people to truly love each other despite their imperfections.

All families have their shadows, and I was finally facing mine.

This was a really, really hard thing to come to terms with, especially because my mom was *dead*. I missed my mom so much. I *loved* my mom so much. What would it mean, if I gave her so much credit for teaching me how to love, how to give, how to be of service, *and* I also felt like sometimes she had hurt me?

I deeply grieve that this is a conversation the two of us will never be able to have, now that I am an adult. That's how it's *supposed* to work. Your parents do their best. Sometimes they make mistakes. Then you get older. Then you get to *talk* about it.

But my mom and I can't. Our story got cut off mid-sentence.

I think both my parents always had the best intentions, but there were a fair number of times when their own stress led to emotional outbursts that affected me when I was younger. I was a very sensitive kid. And that cycle was now playing out again in a different household.

Even though I was currently not in the right headspace to fully process that huge revelation about my childhood, what I did know was that this time was different. This time, I was an *adult*, and these were *not* my parents.

So when I was yelled at, I no longer had to stand there in submission. I was allowed to speak, to communicate my feelings. But it wasn't always taken well.

In June I got kicked out.

I'm not telling you this to paint myself as a victim. We're all only human. My aunt, my uncle, and I, we were all processing a lot of emotions over those few months. COVID was *hard*. Suddenly living together when we never had before, was *hard*. All our lives changed in so many unanticipated ways, and it was a lot to take. I know me being in their home was an unanticipated change and a source of stress, as much as they wanted to help me. I know that processing grief for your sister while her daughter is living under your roof must not have been easy. And I was basically living under their roof as if I was their child, so we naturally all fell into those roles.

But unfortunately, with the headspace that I was in at that time, the way everything happened just compounded all the negative change that I was already struggling to process.

There is nothing and no one that I can rely on.

I didn't know what to do. Face covered in tears, I called my best friend to tell her the news, and she unexpectedly offered up her own home. I moved into her guestroom in July 2020.

Still smack in the middle of the pandemic.

One of my sisters came with me. She was off for the summer and was supposed to join me at our aunt's house, before everything collapsed.

I was still dealing with the move out of my childhood home, and was so grateful to now have my sister there to help me. We drove back and forth, emptying the storage container in my aunt's driveway and moving boxes into my friend's basement.

The basement became our new childhood-memory sorting space. We would spend hours and days on end, sitting on that concrete floor, surrounded by art projects, wine glasses, and family photos. Reducing twenty years of family life down to only the most important keepsakes is no easy task. It wasn't your typical summer vacation.

Living at my friend's house was good … until it wasn't.

It was a simple misunderstanding. But again, we were all dealing with stressors entirely new to us, and trying to adjust to this new COVID-fabricated reality. The conflict ended in miscommunication we couldn't come back from. And it meant my sister and I had to go.

This broke me. My ability to speak, to think, to do anything other than survive, went out the window.

One thing I've come to realize is that none of our life experiences exist in a vacuum. All the situations we encounter are lived based on our *existing frame of perception*. I had been overloaded with So. Much. Change. over the previous year and a half that my mind was just desperately searching for any semblance of predictability. Every time that was broken, my capacity to handle change got lower and lower, until it was on the floor.

Here I was, *again*. I let my guard down, *again*.

Nowhere is safe. I can't rely on anyone. I don't have a home anymore.

No Socks, No Future

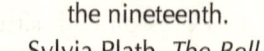

I saw the years of my life spaced along a
road in the form of telephone poles, threaded
together by wires. I counted one, two, three …
nineteen telephone poles, and then the wires
dangled into space, and try as I would, I
couldn't see a single pole beyond
the nineteenth.
—Sylvia Plath, *The Bell Jar*

I made it back to the campus for the beginning of junior year. I was so grateful to have my own space again. My apartment at 202 Wheeler became my home for the next two years.

The address might have finally been stable, but I was an absolute mess.

No one wants me in their life. What is wrong with me?

Why am I expendable?

I was constantly looking for things to fill the void in my chest. I felt life was consuming me from the inside out. I started having a drink every day after class to "take the edge off." I would smoke weed two to four times a week. I ate to numb my emotions and I made a *lot* of online purchases, thinking that maybe one day, when I acquired enough stuff, I would feel whole.

Things got worse halfway through junior year. I began to drown myself in college hookup culture. I was looking for a way to replicate the love that I'd lost when losing my mom, and simultaneously trying to prove to myself that I was *worthy* of being a constant in someone's life.

Hookup culture is actually the *last place* you should go for that.

I would spend time with someone, and after it was over, when I didn't get the feeling of acceptance and love that I was searching for, I would keep searching for that feeling in someone else. I never learned the lesson. There was a point where I was going out to the college bars two to three times a week, and the standards of a "good night" were not based on how much fun I had, but how much attention I was given. I needed alcohol to forget how unhappy I was, and it was incredibly hard to limit my intake. This unfortunately led to multiple blurry nights spent behind closed doors.

Blurry nights led to shameful mornings. One of them still sticks out to me. I woke up dazed and confused, rolling out of an unfamiliar bed, and slowly picked up last night's clothes off an unfamiliar floor. I dressed myself and walked out before the unfamiliar boy woke up.

I blamed myself for not being more careful.

My toes curled in the cold air as I walked down the sidewalk toward my dorm. I couldn't find my socks.

I stayed in a holding pattern from junior into senior year, functioning just well enough to get through classes, do my homework, and then go home and throw myself toward anything and everything I thought could make me feel better, like a girl groping around in the dark for a light switch.

Eventually, my last semester began and college was rapidly coming to a close. "It's time to start thinking about the future!" professors would say.

Future?

It was a foreign concept to me. I had spent all my energy the past four years on surviving.

How can I look forward when I am barely holding on until next week?

In my professional development course we were given an assignment to write out our five-year plan for our career. We had a week to do it.

Everything in me dreaded that assignment. I put it off until the night before it was due, and then eventually made up some standard industry pipeline crap to get the grade. Because I didn't know what I wanted. I didn't know where I was going. When I tried to envision myself five, ten, twenty years into the future, I drew a blank. An absolute, complete blank. I actually couldn't wrap my head around the concept of being that old.

I think, subconsciously, I always thought that I would die young, because I knew that there was no way I could hang on like this forever.

Since I couldn't visualize my future, I had no idea what I was working toward. I was sleepwalking through my own life. So I just kept taking the steps that were directly put in front of me. *Finish the degree, get the first job that comes my way, move up in that field, build the resume, etc ...*

When I finally opened my clouded green eyes, I was a college graduate, living on the opposite side of the country. I had no friends left from my past, and I was stuck in an unfulfilling job that was pushing me further and further toward irreparable burnout.

I wasn't truly living. I was running, sprinting, *killing* myself to overachieve.

What was all of it for?

I didn't know.

All I knew was something had to give.

La Vie en Rose

It's only in fairy tales that princesses can
afford to wait for the handsome prince
to save them. In real life, they have to
bust out of their own coffins and do
the saving themselves.
—Meg Cabot, *Abandon*

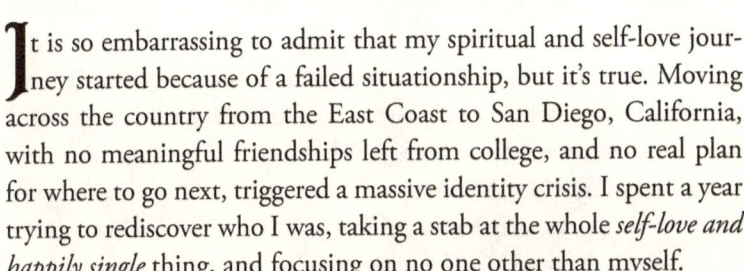

It is so embarrassing to admit that my spiritual and self-love journey started because of a failed situationship, but it's true. Moving across the country from the East Coast to San Diego, California, with no meaningful friendships left from college, and no real plan for where to go next, triggered a massive identity crisis. I spent a year trying to rediscover who I was, taking a stab at the whole *self-love and happily single* thing, and focusing on no one other than myself.

But after a year of not pursuing relationships, I redownloaded Bumble in a low moment one May afternoon in 2023, and went on a date with the first boy who asked me. (Although apparently it wasn't a date? You know how situationships are.)

He lived out of a van and his carefree demeanor was alluring. On our first meeting we walked along the beach, and later that night I sat in his van as he played soft fifties music through his Bluetooth speaker.

I didn't want to go home that night. Being in his presence did something to me. It's hard to describe, but it felt like I could finally breathe.

But his hot and cold communication triggered my anxious attachment style, and after two more meetings, I found myself waiting and waiting for a text back that wasn't coming. Still, I daydreamed of the next time we would see each other. It felt so good when we were together. I *needed* that feeling back. I would try to go about my day, but somewhere in the back of my mind, I was always still waiting for him. That is, until the voice of reason in my head finally resurfaced out of the shadows.

Heather, what are you doing? A year of finally "accepting yourself" and now you're just immediately falling back into the same old patterns? You know better than this. You DESERVE better than this.

The voice was right. I hadn't liked the way I was treated in my college relationships. That was why I took so much time for myself after graduating to figure out my values and priorities, to figure out what I really wanted and not settle for less.

And yet, here I was, settling for the exact same bare minimum, AGAIN!

This boy wasn't shit. There was nothing really there. The dynamics of our relationship were something I did not want for myself. I *knew* that I deserved to be valued, to be someone's priority. And yet, I still couldn't get him out of my mind. I would tell myself I deserved better, but the next day he would reappear from the shadows with a text, and suddenly we'd be hanging out that night.

WHY was I so hung up on him?

I was painfully aware of the cycle I was in, but I couldn't find the strength or the clarity to break it. One day I would have self-respect and the next I found myself begging for his attention.

I laid down on my bed, buried my face into my pillow, and let out a scream.

Why? Why did I need his attention? Why did I need him so much?

I sat up again. Something in him resonated with me. Something in him was fulfilling something I needed, something that I hadn't been giving myself.

What was it? What was it?

I widened my eyes as chills of realization began to travel down my spine.

I wasn't hung up on *him*. I wasn't chasing *him*. The feeling I had when I was with him—that feeling of finally being able to breathe—*that* was what I was chasing. I realized that for the first time in my life, I was experiencing what it felt like to exist outside of fight-or-flight mode, free from the constant stress and tension that had become my normal state of being.

I had never *once* felt comfortable sitting still. I was always moving, always avoiding my own thoughts. Going through so many life-shattering changes that I had absolutely no control over had overloaded the circuits of my brain. I never felt *safe*. I was constantly waiting for the other shoe to drop.

And yet, somehow, this boy's "go with the flow" vibe and the smooth crooning of Nat King Cole out of his Bose speaker had calmed my sympathetic nervous system. It was intoxicating.

I put down my pillow and began to laugh. Everything suddenly made so much sense.

I wasn't addicted to *him*. I was addicted to *being at peace*.

I was chasing a *feeling*.

I've come to find that all we do in this life is chase feelings. We chase the things we think will give us those feelings. We don't want that fancy car; we want to feel important. We don't want that corporate managerial position; we want to feel successful. We're not addicted to substances; we're addicted to the freedom of expressing our true selves without fear of judgment, or we're chasing a reprieve from the darkness within our minds.

The motivation for what we want *always* starts with a feeling. And often, once we get these physical things, we still feel empty inside. We keep grasping for more and more and *more* until the day we finally realize that whatever we *think* we're chasing is an illusion. This boy was the veil over my eyes.

But that day, I understood. I saw the motives behind my actions clear as day, and I finally knew how to break the cycle. The cycle of codependency. The one I'd lived dozens of times over in my friendships, in my relationships, in my family.

I made a decision that day. A life altering decision.

I would no longer put my feelings in the hands of other people.

This boy didn't need to bring me peace.

I could be the one to bring *myself* peace.

So I went back to Ocean Beach.

It was the same beach that I had gone to with this boy, but without the comfort of someone else's shadow to walk in, I felt incredibly exposed.

I wrung my hands together and my shoulders tensed as I tried to take a moment to breathe, to remind myself that I deserved to exist. Even as an adult, I felt I didn't belong in any space I'd ever been in.

Who am I to be on this sidewalk? the critic inside my head kept yelling at me.

As that thought rumbled around my brain, this is what I told myself:

Okay Heather, this is a big city. Absolutely nobody knows you here. And because nobody knows you, you can be whoever you decide you're going to be. So today, you are sure of yourself. Today, you are an actor, and you're going to become a different character. Today, you are playing the role of a confident person.

Walking down the street, I became aware of my hunched posture and the fact that I was staring at the ground.

Act like a confident person, my voice of reason beckoned.

I straightened my spine and looked up toward where I was going, gazing at the end of the sidewalk rather than down.

The perspective shift was profound—I had not realized I had been staring at the ground my entire life.

How long have I lived with lowered eyes, staring at cracks in sidewalks? How much of the world have I missed? How much of my life is passing me by?

As I lay in bed later that night, I smiled to myself. I liked the feeling I got at the beach that day, like I had conquered some years-old mountain created in my mind.

So I kept going back to the beach. Again and again.

I brought my towel and I read books and I listened to a soft fifties playlist. I walked along the rocks as I sang out loud to "Dream a Little Dream of Me" by Ella Fitzgerald. I explored new stores and watched sunsets and hummed and swayed and acted like a confident person … until finally, it started to not feel like a gimmick anymore. It was just how I felt.

Slowly but surely my anxiety was melting away, I was starting to feel at peace, *and* I was becoming more confident.

What was happening here?

I had accidentally stumbled upon the key to releasing the past and becoming your best, most authentic self—that person you were before society taught you to limit yourself, conditioning you to think that you want to be the exact same as everybody else.

It was something that a lifetime of mental health struggles, four therapists, four antidepressants, three stimulants, and two anti-anxiety medications had never been able to do for me.

You can rewire your brain.

Knowing that you can actively change your beliefs and thought patterns puts a wrench in everything you've ever thought about yourself. It did for me. Because now, your identity isn't *who you are*, but rather a *character* that you've created based on your past experiences. Your identity is not fixed, but a *living document*.

This means you have the power to change every single aspect about yourself if you so choose.

But most people won't put in the work to do it. Because it's uncomfortable. Because even if we say we hate being anxious, lonely, reactive, and depressed, those negative beliefs we have about ourselves are familiar. And your brain *loves* to stay in the familiar, like the lumpy dip in your couch from overuse. You might *say* you want a new couch, but whenever you think about buying that firm new cushion, your brain secretly longs for that old familiar slump.

We avoid change like the plague. Your brain will *always* choose a familiar hell over an unfamiliar heaven.

And just because your identity is malleable, doesn't mean change is easy. It is some of the hardest work I've ever had to do. It means delving into your past and digging up those uncomfortable memories that you'd rather keep buried. It means coming face to face with those parts of yourself that you keep locked inside. It means looking honestly at how you have been unconsciously orchestrating every single negative reaction, every self-sabotage in your life.

This is your shadow self. And if you don't learn to control it, *it will control you.*

Everything in this life is hard. Change is hard, but staying in the same negative patterns you've been stuck in for all your life is *also* hard.

I had been miserable for *years*. So I was done running from myself. I knew something needed to change.

I chose my hard. I'm still choosing it today.

And in doing so, I have saved my own life.

THE MUTE

Charlie, don't you get it? ... You can't just sit
there and put everybody's lives ahead of
yours and think that counts as love.
You just can't. You have to do things.
—Stephen Chbosky, *The Perks of
Being a Wallflower*

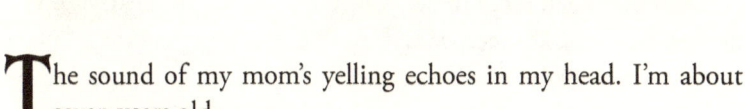

The sound of my mom's yelling echoes in my head. I'm about
seven years old.

I've done something wrong.

I feel ashamed. I was not *trying* to be bad. I open my mouth to
speak, but I'm immediately dismissed with the standard "no talking
back" parental argument.

I stare at the ground, wanting to shrink as small as possible, to
become a speck of dust that could not be seen, not be yelled at.

I was not *trying* to be bad. It was unintentional. If I could just
explain ...

"Look at me when I'm talking to you!"

I force myself to make eye contact and my mind starts to drift
away from reality. I no longer hear words. My vision starts to go
blurry. I just need the moment to be over.

After a few minutes, the lecture ends and I get a reprieve. I go to
my room and cry.

Whenever I used to get yelled at by my parents, I wanted to speak up. Yelling always brought me feelings of shame: *I am a terrible kid, a terrible daughter*.

I so *desperately* wanted to explain my side of the story. I had just made a mistake. I was never *intentionally* trying to be terrible. I *needed* them to know that I wasn't terrible. I just needed to learn how to be *better*. But they never stopped to really listen. I never got the opportunity to speak.

Talking back is rude.

As I got older, it continued. Since I never felt listened to or understood, I had a hot temper and trouble regulating my tone. When I got upset, my voice would start to rise. "Stop whining," became the new dismissal. It was thrown around in the middle of my arguments, cutting me off and immediately ending the conversation. It felt like no one ever listened to what I had to say.

Growing up, I found myself turning into an intense people pleaser. I didn't know what boundaries were. I didn't know how to effectively communicate my feelings. Heck, I didn't even know that my feelings were *valid* enough to be communicated. Any time I had them, I was cut off and sent to my room to process them on my own.

I constantly told myself that I was too much. This belief slowly turned into an unbearable weight. I carried around deep-rooted shame on my shoulders everywhere I went.

This shame and I moved out west to find a job after college, and into another aunt's house in California. Things were calmer here and I lived there for almost a year.

That is until I started going to the beach, rewiring my brain, and pulling myself out of a state of chronic stress.

I realized that what appeared to be a good living situation from the outside, was not good for my psyche, which had been worn down by years of unpredictability. I would be out all day, feeling at peace, and then return home instantly tense. It got harder and harder to pull myself out of the car at the end of the day.

Why do I feel this way? I found myself asking. There wasn't conflict in the house that often.

I soon discovered it was because I was replaying the same home dynamics I had lived three times over. The pattern where I would be hypervigilant, attuned to the needs of the people around me, always waiting for the other shoe to drop. My brain was on overdrive, constantly scanning for changes in tone and heavier footsteps. I just needed to feel *safe*.

I would not speak up for myself, because I feared the possibility of having to move and start over *again*. My feelings and perspective didn't matter to me as long as I could avoid conflict. I was abandoning myself, and it was slowly drowning me. I was telling myself that everyone else's feelings mattered, but not mine. And that is no way to live. In fact, sharing your feelings is the best thing you can do for a relationship, because a relationship where one person speaks on their feelings and the other does not or cannot, *is not a real relationship*.

I knew I had to overcome this fear of voicing my needs and boundaries. It was not fair to expect people to assume my feelings if I didn't communicate them. But voices from the past swirled around in my head …

"Stop whining!"

If I was going to start using my voice, I didn't want to give anyone a reason to silence it. So I began to study how to be a better communicator. I started researching nonviolent communication, and practiced managing my emotions, regulating my tone, validating the other person, making sure to use "I" statements … all the works. I put in so much effort, thought, and time into becoming *better*. Because I just wanted someone to *listen* to me.

The next time conflict arose, I was ready to be respectful, but also say my piece. This would be it. I had learned so much about communication. This time, I would *finally* do it correctly.

It didn't work.

They got upset and left the room, abruptly ending the conversation.

My throat was still full of words left unsaid.

I could feel hot tears welling up in my eyes. I ran out to my car, drove up the street, and parked. I pounded my hands on the steering wheel until I could no longer feel the pain. And then I just started screaming, over and over again, going absolutely feral. It wasn't long before the screams turned to croaking.

I lost my voice. Ironic.

I couldn't believe that this was still happening, even when I was trying my absolute best to be respectful. I had done all the work.

WHY does this keep happening?

I had never been allowed to speak. My past had taught me that *I* was the problem. *I* was the one that made the mistakes. *I* was the one whining. *I* was the one who didn't belong in the home.

I tried so *hard*. I put so much time into becoming better. Into *fixing* myself.

And it had all been for nothing.

I might've been a twenty-three-year-old screaming in her car, but inside I was still just a little seven-year-old girl who wanted to be heard. And she was no longer willing to quiet her voice to keep others' peace at the expense of her own.

Maybe I didn't need *fixing*. Maybe I just needed to *break free*.

I started looking for an apartment of my own.

ONCE UPON A DREAM

"Have you ever been absolutely happy?"
he asked suddenly. "I mean as though the
whole world were an orchestra and instead of
playing more or less off key, for once in your
life you managed to be in complete harmony
and for one day or just maybe for a couple of
hours, everything was exactly right?"
"Yes, once," said Erica.
"Once for me too."
—Gwethalyn Graham, *Earth and
High Heaven*

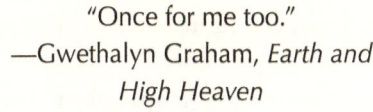

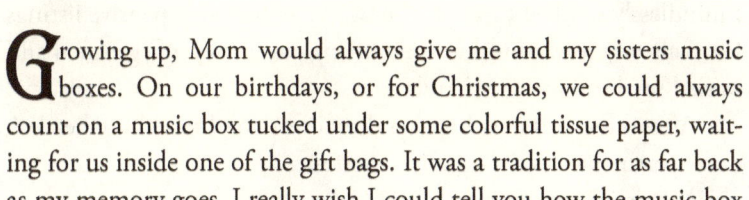

Growing up, Mom would always give me and my sisters music boxes. On our birthdays, or for Christmas, we could always count on a music box tucked under some colorful tissue paper, waiting for us inside one of the gift bags. It was a tradition for as far back as my memory goes. I really wish I could tell you how the music box tradition started, but I can't remember, and Mom is not around to ask.

What I do remember is that every single evening, Mom would come into my room to say goodnight and ask me what music box I wanted to listen to.

A difficult choice—I had a whole shelf of them. As I got older, the one shelf turned into three. Snow globes, figurines, and dolls lined the walls, all with their own unique melody. Over time, I memorized them all.

I would tell Mom my selection for the night, and she would pick up the chosen music box and gently turn the silver dial. The mechanical chimes would start floating through the air. Mom would sit on the end of my bed with me until the melody ended, until the space no longer vibrated with sound. Then she would kiss me goodnight and leave the room.

I felt a special connection to the beach town I had been going to—the one where I first taught myself that I deserved to exist.

Ocean Beach, San Diego.

Now that I was looking for an apartment, I *knew* I was meant to live there. I scanned apartment rentals and roommate posts on Facebook, looking for availability, but I wasn't having any luck.

One gloomy day near the end of June, I was on my lunch break. I mindlessly scrolled through Zillow, the same too-expensive listings I had already seen countless times flying past my eyes. I groaned and buried my head into my hands.

After a few minutes I took a deep breath and raised my head. A new apartment was sitting on the screen.

My *dream* apartment.

It was a roomy studio with rustic cottage vibes in Ocean Beach, and only a block and a half from the ocean. A slight splurge in rent for my budget, but in terms of what it was and *where* it was, an absolute steal.

I called the number on the listing, and six hours later I was standing in that studio, listening to the landlord talk about water heaters and electric outlets.

I returned the next day to hand in my rental application. This landlord operated the old-fashioned way, with paper applications passing through physical hands. As I gave it to him, he told me that as long as he ran the background check and I wasn't a murderer, the apartment was mine.

Oh, and he was also going to lower the rent by $50!

As I walked away, I began to laugh uncontrollably. I stopped in the middle of the sidewalk, shaking with joy and disbelief.

I had never searched for an apartment before, never even handed in a rental application before.

How was that so easy?

A few days later I pulled up to Cape May Avenue with a car full of moving boxes—I was about to meet with the landlord to get my keys.

I turned off my car, excitement and melancholy flowing through my lungs in the same breath.

My first apartment.

This was a big step for me, and I was navigating it completely alone. I felt an emptiness in my chest, one that I had become all too familiar with. The hollow pain tended to pop up alongside all holidays, birthdays, and major life milestones, ever since my After began.

I walked through the emerald green door, and the landlord showed me around the unit for the second time. It was just as I remembered it from a few weeks prior—empty.

Completely empty, except for one item. An item that I hadn't noticed the last time I stood in the room.

This item, my landlord told me, was left from the previous tenant. The previous tenant who had vacated a year before my moving in. Why my landlord chose to leave the item sitting there in that apartment, instead of trashing it or sending it off to Goodwill, is beyond me. But nevertheless, there it was, sitting high up on a shelf.

It was a music box.

Speak Now

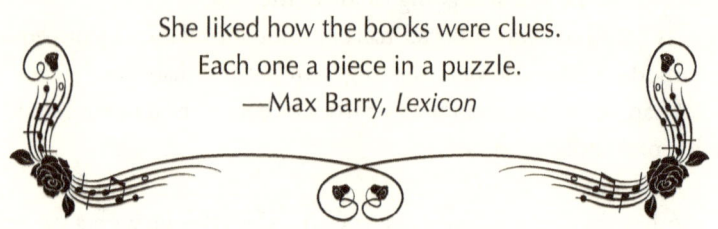

She liked how the books were clues.
Each one a piece in a puzzle.
—Max Barry, *Lexicon*

It was a big adjustment for me, living on my own in my new apartment. In college I had always had roommates or floormates. But now there was no one. I had never had so much time to just sit with myself, to contemplate. In that space, there was a lot of grief.

Something exciting would happen, or I would get home after a long day, and all I wanted to do was call my mom. *ALL* I'd wanted for the past five years, was to dial her number and have her pick up, eager to hear—in that way only moms are—about even the most minute of life updates. It was a luxury I'd never experienced. She was gone before I had started my adult life.

I had some friends I could talk to, but not many. I often felt like my grief strained any friendships I would make, because I relied on them more heavily for emotional support than one normally does in a new connection.

I had my sisters, but they were busy living their own lives. We didn't talk that often, so only reaching out when I was struggling made me feel like I was a burden. I kept my distance.

I had my dad, but we only spoke every few months or so. While on one hand I understood his actions, I was still processing all my own feelings about Mom's death and his decision to move and remarry. I wasn't ready to reach out.

And that's the end of the list. So I started keeping a lot of things to myself.

I began to read to fill the emptiness. That was how I had made it through my childhood—nose in a book rather than feet on solid ground. I preferred to spend my time daydreaming and living in fantasy. The real world was too much. Reading was my escape.

Here, sitting alone in my apartment, nestled into my blue papasan chair, it became my escape once again. I was Alice, falling into Wonderland.

I wasn't made for the real world.

One particular night, the sun had already faded from the sky, and I was cozied up in my chair reading *Pretend I'm Dead* by Jen Beagin. It was a book about a twenty-three-year-old named Mona on a journey to find herself, after a man broke her heart and then passed away from an overdose.

It seemed fitting. The details may have been different, but at the root of it, a lot of my and Mona's pain, grief, and confusion about life were the same.

That night, I was reading a chapter in which Mona met a psychic. This woman was trying to help Mona move past her grief. She told Mona to say her deceased lover's name out loud.

"Names are powerful, Mona. If you utter his name out loud, you'll be able to move on and meet someone else."

You'll be able to move on.

While I personally was trying to come to terms with my mom's death, and not that of a past lover, the sentiment remained the same. Almost five years had passed, and yet I felt like the pain of her loss was just as strong as if it were yesterday. I didn't know what to do to lift this crushing weight of grief that was burying me alive.

So I decided I would say my mom's name out loud in order to try to heal. I actually couldn't remember the last time I had used it—I had always just said "my mom" to people if we *did* talk about her, which wasn't too often either.

Sitting completely alone in my room, I put down my book and told my brain to say my mom's name.

My lips stayed glued shut. My mind was relentlessly sending signals to my mouth, but my mouth wouldn't listen. I eventually got my lips to open, but no sound came out.

I was stuck like that for a few minutes, opening and closing my mouth again and again like a fish out of water. It felt like something was physically blocking my throat and preventing me from speaking.

Why was this so hard?

The more I tried and failed to say her name, the more I realized just how much I clearly needed to. So I continued, determined to break open this Pandora's Box my mind had created around my mom's memory.

I spent a few more minutes opening and closing my jaw like an eager Hungry Hippo. Eventually, though, I was able to push past the invisible force. I spoke my mom's name into existence for the first time in a very long time.

"Laura."

THE YELLOW BRICK ROAD

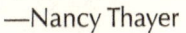

The universe is always speaking to us …
sending us little messages, causing
coincidences and serendipities, reminding
us to stop, to look around, to believe in
something else, something more.
—Nancy Thayer

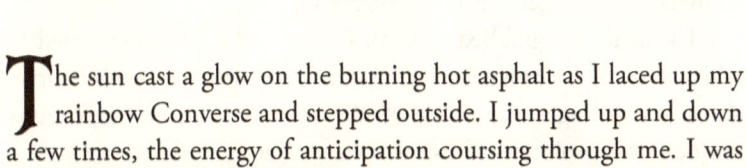

The sun cast a glow on the burning hot asphalt as I laced up my rainbow Converse and stepped outside. I jumped up and down a few times, the energy of anticipation coursing through me. I was on my way to San Diego Pride!

I got on the trolley and made my way toward Balboa Park. Alone.

I had been looking forward to going to Pride for a while, but as the date got closer, I was having a hard time finding someone to join me. I had almost no friends, and the ones I *did* have were busy. I started to panic. I didn't want to miss out.

Then I remembered the rule I had made for myself a month back when I was breaking my cycle of codependency. If I wanted to do something, and no one else could go with me, I would not let that stop me from living my life; I had spent my whole life waiting for people so I could be happy.

My happiness will not depend on other people.

I decided I would go explore the Pride festival by myself. And I would have the time of my life.

Who's to say that I can't do that while also being alone?

I skipped under the massive rainbow balloon arch and couldn't stop the smile spreading across my face. Pride is a place where the outcasts, unicorns, and dreamers thrive.

As I walked past the hundreds of colorful booths, I felt the most myself I had in a long time. I happily stimmed in public—fluttering my hands to the music or shaking a water bottle—without fear of judgment.

Eventually I approached a table run by the San Diego Public Library. Leaning against it was a poster. *What Makes You Proud* was written across the top, with dozens of Post-its pressed underneath in vibrant colors.

I squatted down to eye level and spent a few minutes reading all the little notes people had left. A warm, fuzzy feeling settled into my stomach. The longer I read, the bigger it grew.

I smiled and grabbed a blank Post-it and a pen—I wanted to add my own. Sharpie made contact with paper as I wrote something, something about myself. At the time, I don't even think I fully grasped how profound of a shift it was:

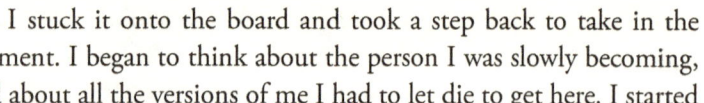

I finally stopped letting other people define who I am ❤

I stuck it onto the board and took a step back to take in the moment. I began to think about the person I was slowly becoming, and about all the versions of me I had to let die to get here. I started beaming. That day was one of the first days I felt truly proud.

Proud to be me.

After a moment I turned away from the colorful board and continued walking down the long line of tents. One in particular caught my eye. I stopped to read the sign sitting out front.

Psychic Readings with Kat.

While I had no idea what I believed about psychics at the time, I had recently decided that stepping into this new version of myself meant trying new things. And I had never been to a psychic before, so *what the hell?* I decided to get a reading.

The skeptic and logical thinker in me also wanted to see how these things worked, to see if I could smell a scam.

I held a crystal in my left hand and extended my right. The woman looked at my palm, studied the tarot cards she had pulled, and began to tell me about my life.

"There are two people," the lady declared after a few minutes. "I'm seeing two people that you've lost in your life. One, you've lost contact with, but the other … the other person is on the other side."

She paused, then began again.

"You've lost your connection with them. They've been trying to get in touch with you. You need to get more in touch with your spiritual side to hear them. Start meditating more."

After this, she spoke for a half hour about a number of other random things, like how I might leave my job soon, and that she saw the infinity symbol surrounding me.

I walked away from the tent without giving all of it much thought.

Yes, I did have one loved one out in the beyond.

But also, that is a pretty *easy* cop out thing to say as a psychic.

A week later, I shielded my eyes from the sun as I drove down Sunset Cliffs Boulevard. The light turned red, and as I rolled to a stop, I noticed a sign posted on the corner of the street.

Estate Sale, it read.

That was it. No address. No hours. Just two words with an arrow pointing left underneath.

I was intrigued. I impulsively pulled into the left turn lane and started following the sign. I made it about a mile down the road until I found another arrow, this time pointing right. I made a right and continued. One more arrow, and I was pulling up to a house.

Various items littered the front yard. I walked up and began looking around—I had just moved into my apartment, so I figured I might find good kitchen supplies.

After vetting the yard I made my way into the house. Mismatched knick-knacks covered the floor and every available surface. I ambled through the downstairs until I came across a bookcase.

If you know anything about me, then you know I have a serious book problem. It's always my favorite part of garage sales. I quickened my pace toward the shelves.

After about a minute, one specific title caught my eye.

Signs, it said.

I pulled the book off the shelf to reveal a baby blue cover decorated with golden branches. A few other symbols—including a dragonfly, a bird, and a compass—surrounded the subtitle: *The Secret Language of the Universe*.

I flipped the book over, my eyes quickly scanning the description on the back cover.

"A renowned psychic medium teaches us how to recognize and interpret the life-changing messages from loved ones and spirit guides on the Other Side."

Communicating with loved ones from the other side?

That psychic's words echoed in my ears. *You've lost your connection with them. They've been trying to get in touch with you …*

I continued reading.

"LAURA LYNNE JACKSON is a psychic medium and the author of the …"

Hold up. *Laura?*

My mom's name.

I stood there, staring at the back of this book for a few minutes, still as stone.

Eventually I broke my trance and went back to looking through the rest of the house, purchased the book and some wooden salad bowls, and began driving home.

Growing up, anytime we passed a sign for a garage sale or an estate sale and we had the time, Mom would pull up to see what we could find. It was something that the two of us used to do together. I had absentmindedly gone and done the same thing that day, even though she wasn't there with me.

But she *was* there with me.

At least that's what it felt like. It felt like her energy was in that house. I'd never felt her presence so strongly.

Energy from the other side? I'd never believed in any of this stuff before. Part of the immense weight of my grief was coming to terms with the fact that as far as I knew, Mom had descended into a vast void of nothingness on September 15th, 2018. Here one moment, and gone the next.

Or was she?

Is the psychic right? Is Mom really out there?

HAPPILY NEVER AFTER

The Magic has come and done it, Becky,
while we were asleep—the Magic that won't
let those worst things ever quite happen.
—Frances Hodgson Burnett, *A Little Princess*

Here's where my story starts taking a much more spiritual turn. I wish I could tell you this cool story of an angel coming to me in a vision, unveiling my eyes to a world beyond ours, but that's not where this chapter begins. It starts as everything apparently does in the era of Gen Z—on Tik Tok.

A video by a woman named Kenzie Swaine appeared on my For You Page. She was sitting under a tree, explaining that each and every one of us has a team of guardian angels. She said that your angels were there to help guide you through life, but they would only intervene if you directly called upon them. Once you did, they would show you a sign that they heard you and were there to help.

I was still in my era of trying new things, and talking to angels *definitely* qualified as a new thing for me. Despite my religious upbringing, I had never been able to believe in forces I could not see with my own two eyes, and proudly proclaimed myself an atheist.

But guardian angels *sounded* cool. I decided to take a stab at it.

I felt a little crazy, but deeper still within my mind was a voice saying, *Why not? What do you have to lose?*

The voice was right. If nothing happened then I just wasted two minutes talking to the ceiling, and I move on with my life.

So I tilted my head toward the heavens, and took a deep breath.

"Hey Guardian Angels. I'm really struggling right now. I'm ready for your help. If you're really up there, could you please send me a sign?"

I felt very silly after doing this.

A few days later, all notions of angels were gone from my head as I collapsed onto my bed, exhausted from work. I picked up my phone and opened Facebook Marketplace—I was looking to buy a dresser. But instead of a piece of polished wood, an event alert popped up on my phone. It was for a garage sale happening at three o'clock, and only a ten-minute walk from my apartment.

I looked at the clock. Exactly three o'clock.

I almost didn't go. I was so tired. But I decided I could use a walk to clear my head, so I dragged myself out of bed and started down the road.

Along the way, I came across a house with the garage door pulled open. A rack of clothes sat on the curb with a $1 sign perched on top. I stopped. I figured I was already on my way to garage sale, might as well look at the clothes too.

As I sifted through blouses and t-shirts, the lady who had organized the sale began talking to me. After a few minutes, she very randomly launched into a story about how she had been on the game show *The Price is Right* a few years ago. She was picked from the live audience to play a game on the show, but she lost and only won $9.

I stopped browsing through the clothes and smiled. This woman's story had sparked an old memory. After she finished, I told her something along the lines of this: "That is so funny that you say that, because growing up in elementary school I used to love watching *The Price is Right* and *Let's Make a Deal* in my kitchen. I used to dream of being on the show and would imagine how good I would do if I went on it."

I kid you not, this lady replies, "You know, I actually got an email two days ago about a casting call for *Let's Make a Deal*. Do you want me to forward that email to you?"

Uhhhhh, yes the fuck I do!

We exchanged contact information, and I walked out of that garage in a daze, thinking to myself, *What just happened?*

Then I looked up. Right in front of me was a tree with a sign tacked to it. I was still on the same block as the game show lady.

The sign was black with white borders on the left and right sides. Inside the borders on the left was a vine of purple flowers, and to the right, silver abstract designs. At the top center, painted in white, was an infinity symbol. Below it were three words:

Be Here Now

Well, that was a sign to me if there ever was one. *And hadn't the psychic mentioned something about an infinity symbol?* I went home and immediately filled out the casting application.

Less than three weeks after that encounter, I was standing in the *Let's Make a Deal* studio in Los Angeles, talking to Wayne Brady on camera.

Things were working out in my favor? My brain couldn't comprehend it. I had created my *entire* adult identity around being the sad girl, the girl who had been dealt a shitty hand, the girl who everyone always leaves.

My story no longer *had* happy endings. My life didn't have any magic. *Stuff like this didn't happen to me.*

And yet it *did*.

Standing on the sidewalk that day in a cloud of disbelief, I found myself thinking back to the angel video, to the half-baked prayer I had spoken into existence only a few days earlier.

Maybe I actually *did* have a team of guardian angels up there looking out for me.

I began to look for more signs, and as I looked, more came. So many signs and synchronicities—some so specific and bizarre— began to appear in front of my eyes. And as this belief in my guardian angels started to solidify, my mind eventually wandered back to the music box that was waiting for me when I moved into my perfect apartment.

If my team of guardian angels was real, was Mom one of them?

The night I had that thought, I looked up to the ceiling again.

"Okay Angels, I'm starting to believe in you. And some of the signs you've been sending are making me think that Mom might be up there with you. So Mom, if you're there, send me another sign."

It came the very next day. For you to understand just how profound this sign was, we have to revisit the worst night of my life.

ETERNAL CLOUDS

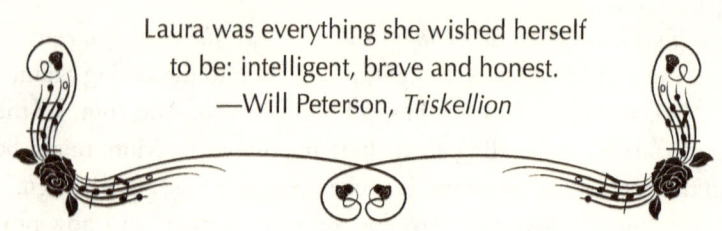

Laura was everything she wished herself
to be: intelligent, brave and honest.
—Will Peterson, *Triskellion*

We got a room. This was not a good sign. Most families got put in the general hospital waiting room. Families with something to cry about got their own room.

My sisters—Jenny and Nancy—and I, sat in a circle, listening to voicemails Mom had left us on our phones.

The first recording on my phone was from 2012. This was back when my SIM card was still in a flip phone. I was in sixth grade, about to be dropped off at summer camp.

I pressed play, and Mom's voice filled the empty space in the white tiled room:

Hi Heather Rosie! It's Mom calling. It's about ten minutes of eleven and I figured Daddy picked you up by now and I was calling just to say goodbye one more time, that I love you … I hope you have a wonderful trip, and stay safe … umm … If you get this message before you go, give me a call back. I'm also gonna try Daddy's phone. Love you! Bye.
Click.

I took a deep breath. It had been a while since I heard her voice.

Mom was still in a coma, and it wasn't looking good. In a few hours she would undergo emergency surgery.

I wanted so badly to stay hopeful, but *we had our own room.*

It was good that we did. The sounds of us losing hope needed to be muffled. I wouldn't want anyone else to hear that pain.

They took her back for surgery around midnight. Dad, Jenny, Nancy, and I walked over to the surgical waiting room. No one else was in there—it was not often they performed surgery this late into the night. I got a bag of Swedish Fish from the vending machine, and we turned on the TV to pass the time. SpongeBob.

After a bit, I laid a blanket on the floor and went to sleep. I was so tired …

I was shaken awake. I will never forget the instant feeling of dread that washed over my entire body.

It's too early. I haven't been sleeping long enough.

I already knew, but I stood there as the doctor told us there was nothing more they could do.

At least my body was standing there. My mind was somewhere else entirely.

This can't be real.

The doctors led us down a maze of hallways and handed us these funny yellow jumpsuits to wear. We pulled the suits over our clothes, a cap over our hair, and booties over our shoes. In any other scenario our appearances would be laughable.

Not this one. The heaviness in the air felt like a trailer truck crushing my chest. I had to make a conscious effort to keep breathing.

They brought us down another hallway and into an open room. Inside sat surgical equipment and machines pushed back to the edges of the walls. About fifteen doctors stood back in a semicircle. Silent, solemn.

In the center of the wide-open space before them was a single metal table. Mom was lying on top of it, arms outstretched, a yellow sheet up to her collarbone.

As I walked closer, I saw her face had started to turn purple.

How is that Mom?

Three weeks ago she was hugging me goodbye at college and telling me she'd see me again, soon.

Now I was the one saying goodbye. Forever.

I leaned down to hug her one last time and kiss her forehead.

I jolted back as if I had been electrocuted. She was already turning cold.

That is not Mom. That is not Mom.

I looked at the floor, at my hands, at the doctors, at the table. I wrung my fingers together into knots so hard my hands began to turn white.

What do you do when the person you love the most in this world is lying dead on a table in front of you?

Floor. Hands. Doctors. Table.

Everything is blurry.

After a few minutes, a voice cut through the crying.

It was Dad. He was singing "You Are My Sunshine."

The room fell still as the soft melody floated through the air. A tear fell down my face, and the last line soon faded into silence.

We filed back out the door and down the hallway. I stared at a fluorescent light panel in the ceiling, as I mechanically pulled the sleeves of my jumpsuit off my arms. My movements felt slow and labored, as if all the blood had been drained from my body.

Our sunshine was gone.

MOMO

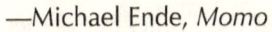

Everything in them was carefully planned and
programmed, down to the last move and the
last moment of time ... But time is life itself,
and life resides in the human heart. And the
more people saved, the less they had.
—Michael Ende, *Momo*

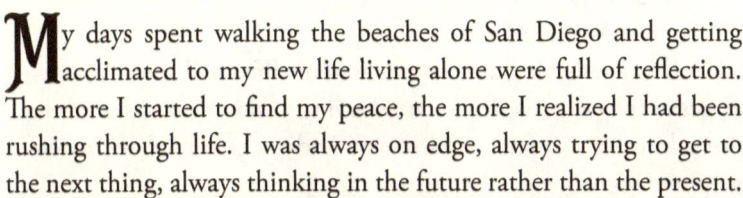

My days spent walking the beaches of San Diego and getting acclimated to my new life living alone were full of reflection. The more I started to find my peace, the more I realized I had been rushing through life. I was always on edge, always trying to get to the next thing, always thinking in the future rather than the present.

It made me reactive. It made me tense. It gave me road rage on the highway, and anger and frustration any time a friend showed up later than our agreed-upon time.

I wandered through life never truly feeling fulfilled, always looking at the clock or the calendar on the wall and wondering where my time had gone.

How did the good things in my life seem to slip by so quickly?

I found myself contemplating what my life would be like if I just slowed down. I had been sprinting my entire life.

What would it be like to just walk forward?

One day as I was musing on all this, a book popped into my head and I couldn't get it out of my mind. *Momo* by Michael Ende.

I had read it back in college for one of my classes.

It was simply a fantasy book, pure fiction—except, as I've come to find, *there is always truth hidden in fairy tales.* Ende's entire made-up world is a metaphor for what capitalism is doing to our perception of time, and therefore humanity.

In the book, the evil Men in Grey from the Timesaving Bank descend upon the city and convince everyone that the way to get to their dream lives is to save time. The newly recruited "time savers" start cutting corners: shortening appointments, stopping unproductive conversations, and cutting out inessential activities like hanging out with friends and sitting in reflection at the end of the day.

These people saved their time, but as they did, their life flashed before their eyes. Because if you spend your whole life rushing and trying to save time, you can never stop to actually *live* it.

This book lingered in the back of my mind for weeks, whispering out its name to me.

Momo, Momo, Momo.

I began reflecting on how much of my life I had spent just trying to get to the next chapter. I started trying to slow down, even though everything in our fast-paced society had programmed me to never stop moving.

The day I got a sign from my mom was one of these days.

I had the day perfectly planned out to the minute. I got off work at noon. After that, I would drive over to a neighboring town to pick up a pair of purple rollerblades I was purchasing from Facebook Marketplace. I would get there by 12:20 p.m., then drive back home with enough time to find street parking before meeting my friend Morgan at my apartment at 1:00 p.m.

But that is not what happened.

I finished my shift, walked into the parking lot right on the dot of noon, and pulled out my phone. There was a new message from the Facebook seller. She was so sorry, but she was running late. Could we push the meeting time back by fifteen minutes?

I immediately started to get reactive. My brain freaked out, telling me to respond and say never mind, let's just do it another day. Or even better, tell her I actually don't need the rollerblades at all, and forget about the whole thing.

Momo, Momo, Momo.

I caught myself. I was doing that thing that I *always* do, where I try and try to save time and I end up impatient, unhappy, and I often self-sabotage.

I decided I wasn't going to do that this time. I knew that even though I was scheduled to hang out with Morgan soon, she likely wouldn't be on my doorstep right on the dot of 1:00 p.m.

I could *afford* to be patient today.

So I sat in my car and waited a few minutes. I decided to use the opportunity to pay my gas and electric bill that I had been putting off for days, but knew would take less than five minutes to complete.

A few taps on my phone, and a green check mark appeared. Paid!

Why did I keep putting that off and stressing myself out when it only took two seconds?

I pulled out of the lot and began making my way to the seller's house.

I had only spoken to my angels out loud once or twice at that point. It still seemed very foreign to me, and I still felt a bit crazy, but as I drove down the highway, I decided to do it again.

I was excited at the pattern I had just broken; I wanted to tell *someone*.

"Hey Angels, did you see what I just did there? Because in the past I always get so impatient, and try to plan out every last thing, and when it doesn't go according to the plan, I freak out. But I *didn't* do that this time. Are you proud of me?"

I finished speaking into the void and continued rolling down the highway. After a few more minutes, I glanced at my phone for the directions. I saw the exit I was supposed to get off at, and then my phone instantly went dark—it had overheated from sitting on the dash in the hot sun.

Normally I would get frustrated, exasperated at this setback.

Momo, Momo, Momo.

Instead, I took a deep breath. I gave thanks for the fact that I saw my exit right before the phone turned off. I took that exit and turned off into the first gas station. Then I sat patiently, waiting for my phone to turn back on.

It's okay, everything happens for a reason. You are meant to be here, a voice in my head assured me.

Soon enough my phone came back to life and I continued on my way. I made it to the rollerblades, paid the woman on Venmo, and started on my way back home again.

I have always loved the color purple, because Mom loved the color purple. Driving home, I was on a high—I was really excited about my *purple* rollerblades.

I cruised down the street, but as I approached the left turn onto the highway ramp, the light turned yellow.

If I sped up I could probably *just* make the light. And that's what I usually did. I was always *rushing*.

Momo, Momo, Momo.

I slowed to a stop. I was starting to embrace the idea of divine timing.

It's fine. You're in no rush. You were just meant to be at this light.

No sooner had I thought that, than a car pulled up to my right. I looked over and saw a small sticker on the side window near the backseat.

Have a little faith, it read. Faith was written in purple.

Hmmm, I thought to myself. *Nice encouragement. The purple makes me think of Mom.*

I pulled out my phone and snapped a picture. Immediately their light went green again and the car sped off. As it rolled away, I noticed there was one other small sticker, this one sitting on the car's rear window.

You are my sunshine.

There was my sign. I had almost forgotten I had asked for it.

I started sobbing as I turned onto the highway. Tears streamed down my face while the song that was playing from my phone ended and a new one began.

It was "Mama" by NF. NF had lost his own mother and created this song as a tribute. The tears fell harder as I listened to the lyrics, asking if she had found happiness and peace up in heaven.

My face was wet with emotion as I exited the highway and turned onto the street my apartment was on. Immediately a blue Honda Odyssey rolled through the intersection in front of me and was gone.

A blue Honda Odyssey—the car my mom drove when I was growing up.

I cried harder.

I began to slowly cruise down the street. It was a Saturday—a day notoriously hard to find street parking. But as I drove along, there was one spot waiting for me.

As soon as I parked, I called Morgan. She picked up the phone halfway through the first ring.

"You have perfect timing."

Chills traveled down my spine.

What is going on?

Morgan had been meeting with some other friends in the area and had just finished. From what she told me, she said goodbye to her friends, got into her car, and pulled out her phone. And there I was, already calling her.

I think it was around 1:30 p.m. at that point. We were supposed to meet at 1:00 p.m. But we had both *surrendered* to the moments that we were in, to what life had presented us at that point in time. And somehow in doing so, we had still finished at the *exact same time*.

Perfect timing.

I got back to my apartment and started freaking out—running around in circles, jumping up and down, and peering out the window waiting for Morgan to come. So much had just happened in the past hour, and I needed to get it off my chest or it felt like I would explode.

Eventually, I saw a familiar mop of ginger blonde hair traveling down the street. As soon as Morgan stepped through the door, I began relaying the day's events to her. I started describing the magic that occurred when I decided to slow down, be patient, lose track of time …

I screamed, catapulted myself onto the floor, and started rolling around. I didn't know how else to convey the gravity of *what-the-fuckery* I was experiencing in that moment.

Morgan stared at me with concern in her eyes.

"Are you okay?" she asked, confused.

I tried to take a second to collect myself, but all I could utter from my fetal position on the ground was, "You're the name of the book!"

Morgan's childhood nickname was *Momo.*

She was the name of the timesaver book.

Morgan and I were planning to meet that day to make my costume for *Let's Make a Deal,* but this situation derailed us. The glue gun sat there cold and the craft supplies unopened.

We ended up going down a deep rabbit hole. We had this amazing conversation about life, about unexplainable coincidences, about grief and dealing with loss.

It was one of the best conversations I'd had in a long time. Too often, we can get so caught up in the trivial details of life. But this was what I had been longing for, all those times in the past five years when I was struggling to make meaningful connections with others.

A soul conversation.

Eventually, I broke the trance and looked at my phone. A few *hours* had passed.

We had lost track of time, and we hadn't finished what we had set out to achieve that day. But what we got was much greater.

A memory that can last a lifetime.

Losing track of time.

As I sat in my apartment that night and reflected on the day's events, I realized that *that* was the key to life. The key to rediscovering our humanity.

"Time is money," they say. Every moment is an opportunity! And every second that passes where that opportunity is not seized, becomes a *second wasted.*

I had been taught to believe that my life was a numbers game. I had stopped looking at my life as the true gift that it was, but as a math equation. More time equals more earning potential. And so I rushed, I excessively planned, and I missed the magic right in front of me.

I know that we need money to live, but I do not think that that is the meaning of life. If money equaled freedom, then everyone with a good job would be free.

True freedom is freedom of *time*.

Once I slowed down, I began to see my life for the miracle that it was. It was in the small moments. The conversation I had with Morgan. My neighbor recognizing me from across the street as I rode my bike, exchanging a wave and a smile. The mouth-watering creaminess of avocado. Singing and dancing as I scrubbed the dishes, relearning how to find joy in my life. Reading a quote in a book that spoke directly to my soul.

That is what truly matters to me. Jobs, careers, and money are a *means to live*. We are all programmed into thinking that they are our *reason for living*. And so we have lost ourselves. We have lost our patience, kindness, compassion, and humanity, in order to save time.

Only in slowing down did I start to see the magic in my life. Only in slowing down did I start to become grateful for what I had and everything I was blessed with. Only in slowing down was I able to have the most profound day of my life, discovering that my mom was still out there, watching over me from beyond.

I had spent so much of my adult life drowning in the past or worrying about the future. But my life is *NOW*. And I was going to do whatever I needed to do to actually start *living* it.

I will not waste any more of my time.

GOLDEN HANDCUFFS

I just mean, Glinda, is it possible we could be
living our entire adult lives under someone's
spell? How could we tell if we were the
pawns of someone's darker game?
—Gregory Maguire, *Wicked*

My life was getting a little better. I was beginning to heal. But not all my demons lay inside—some of them took the shape of a fancy corporate job.

To the untrained eye, my life probably appeared to be going pretty well. Even though I had struggled with my mental health throughout college, I had landed a job with a local news station in San Diego only three months after graduation. And eight months later, I got a new job. Same job description. Different, more reputable news station. Fifty percent pay raise. Photojournalist at ABC News, San Diego!

My first full-time salary. Benefits. The *dream*. And I was finally starting to step into a more confident version of myself. Life *must* be going well.

Nope. I was miserable.

I felt completely isolated in the corporate space. It didn't feel natural to me. It felt like I was working two jobs: the actual job I was being paid to work, and the social labor of trying to figure out how to put on a mask and mold myself into what this company wanted me to be. It felt like everyone around me was speaking a completely different language. And I was hyperaware of the fact that when I went out into the field, I was not only representing myself, but the ABC establishment as a whole.

I hated it. I didn't feel professional. I didn't feel good enough. I felt like an actor being forced to play a role that I wasn't meant to be cast in.

I spent my workdays terrified of making a mistake, overworking and overstressing myself to compensate for that fear. I was thrown into situations I didn't have the emotional capacity to handle. Interview someone who just lost their husband or their one-year-old child? All I could do was spend the whole time thinking about losing my mom and how talking to a reporter would be the *last* thing I would want to do in that situation. And yet *I* am supposed to impose myself on others?

There was also no stability. My work week started at 2:30 a.m. on Saturdays. 3:30 a.m. on Sundays. 7:00 a.m. Monday through Wednesday. My schedule was inconsistent, unorthodox, and incredibly difficult to adjust to both mentally and physically. As an adult, *all* I had ever needed was a predictable, stable environment.

My brain had no time to rest. I was burnt out and overwhelmed, spending my days walking around with a twenty-pound camera. This only exacerbated the chronic pain I've had since I was seventeen—a result of my hypermobility and high stress levels. I couldn't move without pain radiating down my neck and shoulders. I would get home and not have the energy to do anything but lie in bed. All my time home was spent recharging for the next time I would be back on the clock. My life became work and nothing else.

The more and more I reclaimed my peace, the more aware I became of just how good this job was at stealing it. I was finally learning to take control of my brain, and the hustle, high-stakes, and emotional overwhelm of the news was pulling me right back down again.

I kept thinking to myself, *Is this all there is?* I spent my whole life wanting to grow up, but being a "grown-up" was *drowning* me. People had been at the station I was working at for ten, twenty, thirty *years,* waiting around for their vacation days and scrambling to submit time-off requests. Two months in and I was already beginning to blow through my own vacation days—in bed trying to ensure I was rested enough to still be able to work. I knew that I could not endure this for the next forty years. Heck, I didn't think I could last even another *month.* But I didn't know what I wanted. I didn't know what to do. I felt stuck. It felt like this was just what adulthood was and I had to learn to deal with it.

Until, I woke up one day with that little voice in my head again.

Quit your job, quit your job, quit your job.

The voice had never been so insistent before. I couldn't get it out of my mind. It wasn't coming from a place of stress or fear. It was coming from a place of *knowing.* It just felt right.

Quit your job.

This voice, combined with reaching my breaking point of mental exhaustion from work, had me spiraling into a deep reflection on everything I had ever tried to work toward in life, and the things I had thought that I wanted.

And for the first time, I realized that none of it actually *mattered* to me.

I found myself thinking, *What have I been doing? What is all this for? Why am I here?*

And not just here at this job, but here on *earth.*

I realized that my entire life, I had not been moving with intention. I had just been a cog in the system. It felt like I had been sleepwalking for years and was just now waking up.

I would walk down the street and wonder how my perspective had so radically shifted. I would stare at racks of clothing, in shock about just how much money I had spent in the past, thinking fancy clothes would bring me happiness. I would drive past fast-food bill-boards and think to myself, *How have I spent so long craving this stuff? That isn't real food.* I would pass bars and think about how much money and time I had spent pursuing the bottom of a glass, just to realize that it didn't leave me feeling anything real.

Everything in the world was the same, and yet it was entirely different.

Snapchat, billboards at every turn, get-rich-quick schemes in every other video on Instagram reels, ChatGPT, alcohol at every event, grids upon grids of buildings, people glued to their phones and not looking up—my brain became inundated with all of these things as if I was experiencing life for the first time. Not only experiencing it, but realizing that *all of it was meaningless.* These things only had meaning because we, as a society, had *decided* that they meant something.

We *decided* that owning Louis Vuitton and Gucci and Nike Air Force Ones were an indicator of status. We *decided* that a job working for a well-known company automatically made you successful in the eyes of other people.

I had been following it *blindly.* But all these manufactured meanings no longer held value to me, no longer held control over me. It was as if I unlocked a new level of self-awareness. It was overwhelming and isolating. I felt like Neo, waking up inside the harvesting pod and ripping the cords of control out of his body.

I was waking up to the matrix.

It suddenly made sense why everything that I *thought* would make me happy in life had gotten me nowhere. It was because it wasn't what I *actually wanted.*

It was *societal conditioning.* It was what I had been *programmed* to want.

I didn't know who I was anymore, or what I *really* wanted. I reflected on my job and realized that I was only staying in it for the money, and I was no longer willing to sacrifice my happiness for *any* job.

What now?

In the past I had been living my life so attached to myself and my own mind, completely unaware of other people. Now I felt a deep-rooted call to help people, to give back to the world. I didn't know how yet, but I did know that I couldn't figure it out while I was so burnt out that I was struggling to meet my own basic needs.

Time to start over.

THE LIGHTHOUSE

Her future looked impossibly bright.
And then—she quit.
—Laura Lynne Jackson, *Signs: The Secret
Language of the Universe*

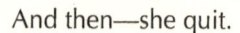

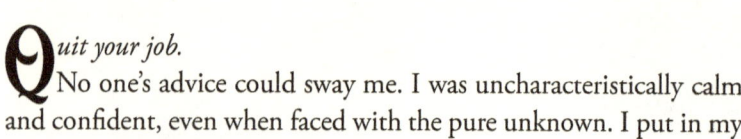

Quit your job.

No one's advice could sway me. I was uncharacteristically calm and confident, even when faced with the pure unknown. I put in my two week notice two days later.

In the past I had made super impulsive decisions without properly thinking them through. This had been Heather in survival mode—acting out of fear, desperately trying to grasp onto something, anything.

But this time was different. This was the first decision I made as just Heather. I realized that the little voice in my head that I had started to follow was my intuition, guiding me toward my highest path.

The reality is I had already hit severe burnout while working part-time at the first news station. I was doing terribly, and my brain fog was getting so severe that I was losing my ability to function. I reached out to different family members, telling them how scared I was getting. I even started to research filing for disability. But everyone just kept telling me, "You need a job. You need to have another job lined up before you quit. You need to make money."

So, scared and desperate for a quick way out, I applied for the same exact position at what I thought would be a better company. I was a fish jumping out of polluted water into yet another murky pond, because of others' fears surrounding money and what I would do if I didn't have a job.

Since I didn't take time to recover from my burnout, it compounded at this new job. I dragged myself to work and then back home to sleep. I reached a point where it felt like I wasn't even conscious, even though I was fully awake—I was spacing out and losing entire moments of time in my memory. One minute I would be standing in the break room, and the next I was in the locker room, eyes lazily scanning the tripods stacked in the corner, brows furrowed in confusion—an hour had passed. I became terrified about this happening while out in the field where I needed to keep my instincts sharp for my own safety, or worse, while driving.

I knew something needed to give. The voice in my head only confirmed what I already knew I needed to do internally. I just had been too terrified of the unknown to entertain the idea or even voice it out loud before.

I didn't know exactly where I would go next, but I knew that where I was wasn't sustainable. There was no other way. I needed a break to recover, to reteach myself how to live, and to figure out what I was meant to do in this life because this wasn't it.

So I decided to leave with no plan. I decided to take some time to heal. I decided that I could always get a job waiting tables if I needed money while I was still finding my direction.

What others may look at as an irresponsible decision, I view as the most responsible decision I've ever made. I was forcing myself to take responsibility for fixing and pursuing a better life, because I knew my current life was on a rapid crash-and-burn trajectory, even if those around me could not see it at the time. And not having a source of income would *force* me to work toward finding a job that aligned with my values and my health, or risk turning around and walking right back into the hell I dragged myself out of.

So I took a leap of faith and quit my job. I was there for three months.

How's *that* for a resume boost?

My sisters did not agree with my decision to quit. They have always been the by-the-book, follow-set-plans type, on their way to becoming doctors.

All power to them, but that's never been me.

It was absolutely terrifying, the day I was on the phone with one of them and said, "It's okay that you don't agree with my decision. It's still my decision to make and I *know* it's the right one."

My voice wobbled as I hung up the phone. I knew that the only proof I had that what I had just said was true, was my own faith and confidence in myself—confidence that was still wavering behind closed doors.

I also couldn't really explain to them the voice in my head, the signs I'd been getting from Mom, and the rapid perspective shifts I was undergoing—they would've told me I was a crazy person. So I let them think I was an irrational, impulsive person instead.

One day as I was hashing it out on the phone with one of my sisters, one of the things she told me was, "Being an adult means doing things you don't want to do."

That phrase stuck with me for a while, playing endlessly over and over in my head like a broken cassette tape.

"Being an adult means doing things you don't want to do."

No, it absolutely does not!

Why do we think that way? Who gave us that belief? Why are we all so programmed to believe that adulthood equals suffering? That in order to live we must endure?

I *refuse* to believe that's what life is. I believe that we create our reality. I believe that if you operate under the belief that being an adult means doing things you don't want to do, you will continue to attract those experiences. And I believe the idea that as an adult you must endure your job, is a mindset perpetuated by corporate America to keep the majority of people working at the bottom, generating wealth for someone else without complaining. When we sit in that mindset, we become a slave to our own minds.

Call me delusional, but I was done living in my own mental prison.

This situation raised some deep philosophical questions for me. What is "adulthood" as we think of it? What do I want my adulthood to look like? What if adulthood was *fun*?

What would it take for me to feel successful?

I remembered a family gathering two weeks prior to quitting my job, in which an uncle told me he was so proud of me for getting that job and being where I was.

A year out of college, and I was already a photojournalist at ABC News? Outstanding!

But when he said that, my stomach began to twist into knots. Something felt off to me. It took me a little while to realize why.

It was because *I wasn't proud of myself.*

I had always gone with the grain, but it wasn't what I really wanted. It was what I had been *conditioned* to want. I couldn't believe I had never realized it before.

Success is an *individual* concept. Happiness is an *individual* concept.

In college, I was in such a dark headspace that I was absolutely *terrified* of getting stuck in that place forever. So I tried to get out of it by pursuing the things that other people had told me would give me success and happiness—accolades, fancy-looking jobs, relationships. But none of that had gotten me *anywhere*.

I wasn't living life for me. I was living life according to the predefined plan society engrains in us as children. The American Dream. A salary job, marriage, kids, and a white picket fence.

It never sat right with me.

Regardless of the fact that our economy is changing, and that dream is becoming harder and harder to attain, that is *someone else's* dream. It's not *mine*. And it's absolutely fine if that *is* your dream, but every person needs to really look inside and decide for themselves.

What do I really want? What does my version of success look like?

It was hard to come back with an answer. I had let the pressures of society, of family, of what I thought I "should" do, define it for me for too long.

But then I remembered the central truth I had uncovered when I was trying to stop obsessing over that guy in his van on the beach.

We don't chase things, we chase feelings.

I grabbed my notebook, sat down on my couch, and began to imagine my dream life. But here's the catch: I could not describe physical items, things, jobs, etc. I limited myself only to feelings and concepts. After a moment, I put pen to paper and began to write:

> *I want to help people, to feel like I'm giving back somehow. I want to share my ideas because I know I have valuable things to say. I want to create a community that lifts each other up. I want to have time freedom and feel like I am the one in control of my own life. I want to feel like the work I am doing is building toward something bigger. I want to feel at peace. I want to stop being in a rush all the time. I want to be intentional with my work. I want to turn the knowledge I've gained from my negative experiences into something positive.*

I put my pen aside and stared down at my notebook. There were some dots to connect here.

At peace, not in a rush, intentional.

Apparently hustle culture and the news industry could *not* be more misaligned! No wonder I was miserable.

Time freedom, in control, building something.

Maybe I'm meant to be my own boss.

Turn my knowledge into something positive, share my ideas, help people, give back, create community.

I needed to use my knowledge to help people in some way. How could I do that?

Maybe you should become a spiritual coach.

The voice was right. I didn't know how I knew, but I knew.

From budding photojournalist to spiritual coach? The people in my life who witnessed this complete 180 in real time were baffled and confused.

I had nothing I could say to them. The pull to become a spiritual coach was so strong and so unexplainable that it almost felt like I didn't pick it for myself, the universe picked it for me.

Even when the idea first came into my head, I don't think I was fully equipped to enter into the role. But I was immediately thrown into more life situations that gave me the knowledge and wisdom I needed to move forward.

I've since learned that this is how the universe works. You declare an intention, and then the universe will throw *everything* in your path in order to prepare you for it.

And once the seed was planted in my brain, that was it. I've always loved giving advice and been told that I was wise beyond my years. My experience with many different difficult life experiences had given me a massive life perspective shift, and I always got a huge spark of joy any time I shared something I learned and it helped others through their own troubles.

I wanted to help people find peace and happiness, help people unlock the tools they already have inside themselves to achieve everything they want, help them fall in love with the journey, and truly live in the moment. And at the root of it all, I wanted to be that safe space, that emotional stability for others that I had spent my life searching for. That was what would make me feel fulfilled.

My intuition led me to this career. I had found my soul's path.

For the past twenty-three years, I was wandering around in the dark, slowly figuring out life lessons by endlessly bumping into walls and tripping over cracks. Now, battered and bruised, I had finally stumbled upon a door with all the answers.

But imagine if you had someone actually guiding you—putting bridges at your feet to get you over the cracks they've already broken their ankle in, telling you what bumps to avoid, and shining a light to point you toward your own door to happiness and fulfillment.

I want to be a lighthouse. To guide the lost souls home.

Holy Guacamole

But it is vitally important that you stay alert.
Coincidences will occur regularly, but you
have to notice them. Do you understand?
—James Redfield, *The Celestine Prophecy*

I was slowly counting down the August days until the end of my job. By the time I decided to leave, I had already reached my breaking point. When someone spoke to me, it took a good ten seconds to process what they were saying, and I spent all my breaks in a room alone with the lights off because I couldn't handle any form of stimulation. Doing any task took everything I had left in me. But I didn't want to leave on bad terms, so I dragged myself to work for the next two weeks before officially leaving.

It was difficult being caught in between my old life and my new one—stuck in the old paradigm, but knowing I was meant for more.

I listened to the usual musings and complaints of my coworkers that I used to partake in. But now, I just felt like I was trapped in *Groundhog's Day*. This couldn't be what life was. I needed to get out. I needed to break free.

Just fourteen days.

One of those final days, I was driving back to the news station from a film assignment, about to take my lunch break. I had almost made it back—only two turns from the entrance—when I decided I needed a sandwich. I hadn't had time to bring lunch that day, and I didn't think my granola bar was going to cut it.

I put "sandwich" in Google Maps, clicked the closest result, turned the car around, and started driving.

This was a bit impulsive of me, but if I had learned anything from the purple rollerblade scenario, it was that *magic happens when you break out of your patterns.*

I showed up on the corner of a mini mart. It was one of those small grocery stores with a deli at the back. I walked up to the counter and ordered a sandwich. It was a vegetable sandwich, stacked with guacamole, cheese, sprouts, peppers, spinach, onions, and tomato.

This was also out of the ordinary for me. I used to go for pasta, meat, and unhealthy snacks. Carbs and sugar were my best friends— I'd always been vegetable averse. But for the past couple of weeks, I found myself craving things like raw carrots and food grown straight from the ground. I didn't know what was happening to me.

The employee took down my order, and then I took a step back. As I waited, I glanced down the nearby aisle. My eyes settled on a group of candles sitting on the shelf. I was curious, and still waiting for my sandwich, so I walked over to them.

It was a group of prayer candles. And smack dab in front of my face was a prayer candle that said *Guardian Angel* on it. I smiled in disbelief.

I had only ever seen prayer candles at vigils once or twice in my life. I wasn't familiar with them at all. I didn't know where one would usually buy them. And this was a really small mini mart. It was mainly just full of groceries and some other convenience items.

And prayer candles? Seemed a little odd—I wanted to have a conversation with their stock guy.

I had worked at ABC for two and a half months at this point, and had never been to this deli, which was only five minutes away. I also had no plan to get a sandwich, and then suddenly my brain thought, *You know what? Sandwich.*

And now I was staring at a guardian angel candle.

I walked up to the cashier—sandwich in one hand, guardian angel candle in the other, and my official press badge still hanging around my neck.

I have to admit, I felt a little less than sane in that moment.

HEATHER ROSIE

She had opened her mind to the words the way
an eye used to darkness, veiled with its lashes,
opens cautiously to the light, and, finding it even
a little blinding, closes itself too late. The light had
come, and come invincibly, even after the eye had
renounced it. It was too late to unsee.
—Hannah Green, *I Never
Promised You a Rose Garden*

The week I was supposed to go to Los Angeles to film for *Let's Make a Deal*, it felt like the energy in the air had shifted. I was starting to look at the world around me through rose-colored glasses. I knew getting cast on this show was the work of my angels, sending me on a new adventure. And it wasn't lost on me that this adventure involved traveling to the *City of Angels*.

I decided to book a hotel so I could have a free day to explore after filming. It felt like something I was supposed to do. It felt like there was something waiting for me to discover.

Usually spending a free day in a new city would mean research-ing and planning tourist destinations, but instead I threw all plans and expectations out the window. On the drive up I asked the angels to provide me with guidance on how to spend the afternoon after filming the show, as well as the next day—I was getting increasingly more comfortable speaking to them out loud.

The day of filming, I made friends with one of the other contestants, Zulema. I walked up to a group of people when I heard a girl with caramel skin and short curly ebony hair speaking about manifestation, so I started telling her about my crazy angel story that got me onto the show. We clicked instantly, and when I mentioned I had the rest of my day free after filming, she said she did too and that we should hang out!

After she said that it dawned on me …

Let's Make a Deal was a *costume* show. And Zulema had dressed up as *roller skating Barbie*. Immediately after she said she was free to hang out that afternoon, my eyes widened as I glanced at the trunk of her car behind her.

The trunk where her *purple roller skates* were sitting.

I swear my angels are up in the sky working overtime.

We decided we just wanted to hang out in a park and talk, so we pulled up a map of Los Angeles on our phones and started looking at all the green patches we could see in our area. Closest to us was a splotch of green on the map bigger than all the others. I pinched my two fingers to zoom in closer. It turned out this giant piece of land was not a park at all, but a cemetery—Forest Lawn Memorial Park.

"Oh okay no, let's find a different park," Zulema said immediately.

I know I should've agreed with her, but something in my mind was drawing me toward Forest Lawn. I couldn't explain it, but the pull was there. I continued to zoom in closer, hesitantly scanning the vast expanse of green, until I came across a church sitting in the middle of the grounds.

It was called Wee Kirk O' the Heather.

I narrowed my eyes as I reread the words on the screen.

A church with *my* name? I'd never seen that before. And I had felt mysteriously drawn to the park, even before finding that church on the map.

Odd.

I brushed that moment off, and Zulema and I spent the rest of the evening together getting to know each other.

In a normal park. One that wasn't full of dead people.

I woke up the next morning with a whole free day ahead of me in Los Angeles to explore.

How should I spend it?

The normal side of my brain was telling me to go to the beach. Browse the Santa Monica Pier or the Hollywood Walk of Fame. Do something like a normal person.

But a deep, unexplainable, mystical part of my brain was saying, *Go to the church, go to the church, something is waiting for you there.*

Against all common sense, I got in my car and began making my way toward Forest Lawn Memorial Park. It was as if an invisible rope was pulling me there. I was an unsuspecting soul, following the siren call and blindly walking toward the light.

I pulled up to the entry gate and asked for directions to Wee Kirk O' the Heather. It was a much larger property than I expected—around 300 acres. As I drove away from the booth, the absurdity of my current situation fully landed on me. Here I was, a twenty-three-year-old woman, spending my one free day in Los Angeles visiting a giant cemetery and pulling up to random churches because I had an undeniable voice I couldn't get out of my head.

But there it was again. *Something is waiting for you there.*

I had to know. I had to know what was on the other side of this calling.

I drove on.

I ascended a hill, and the greenest grass I had ever seen cascaded down the slopes on either side. I drove past glistening pools of clear water and beautiful white marble statues. The air was serene, and the sun cast a heavenly glow over my cherry red Mazda.

This was no cemetery. Any cemetery I had been to was a dreary-seeming place. This was paradise. A proper resting place for lost souls.

I approached a small brownstone building nestled into some trees, and I pulled over and turned off my ignition. There were no other cars or people around. The world had never felt so still as it did in this place.

Something is waiting for you there.

I got out of my car and walked up to this church, unsure of what I would find, but having a deep inner knowing that I was meant to be there. As I stood in front of the doors, I gasped. There was a sign there etched into the stone. It said:

**WEE KIRK O' THE HEATHER
FOREST LAWN MEMORIAL PARK
RECONSTRUCTION OF ANNIE LAURIE'S CHURCH
GLENCAIRN, SCOTLAND**

A warm feeling spread throughout my chest. My Mom's name was Laura, so one of her nicknames growing up was Laurie. Here I was, visiting a church with *my* name, but I wasn't expecting my *mom's name* to be involved as well. Not to mention the fact that this Heather church was built in the Annie Laurie church's image.

The metaphor there was striking.

There was a giant wall to my left with the history of Annie Laurie's Church. I started reading. It turned out that it was a non-denominational church. This made me feel a bit more comfortable, as I did feel a bit uneasy being at a church again. Due to my conflicting feelings as a child growing up in both a Catholic and an Evangelical Christian church at the same time, I identify as a spiritual being without ties to any specific religion.

After I finished reading the history of Annie Laurie, I walked over to the doors and pulled one of the large ornate handles.

Locked.

The voice was wrong this time.

I'm not going to lie, I was a bit bummed. I thought there was something there for me to find. But I was still enjoying the experience of exploring and looking at things with a fresh, curious mind. So I turned and walked around the back of the building.

I came to a small iron gate. Next to it was a sign:

THIS LITTLE GARDEN HAS BEEN RESERVED FOR THOSE OF YOU WHO DESIRE TO DRAW APART AND REST AWHILE IN SILENT MEDITATION AND PRAYER. SIGHTSEERS WILL PLEASE NOT ENTER THIS GARDEN BUT RETRACE YOUR STEPS AND VIEW THE GARDEN FROM THE VESTRY WALK.

I had just recently started to tap into the power of meditation—I was trying to listen to the advice the Pride psychic had given me—so I decided that I would go and meditate in this garden.

I slowly pushed the gate open while it groaned back in protest. Cobwebs fell away from the rusted railings.

And then I entered another world.

The energy of this garden was so serene that I could feel the distinctive shift. Straight ahead of me was a fountain, water slowly trickling out of the mouths of four lion heads. I stood there for a few minutes, getting lost in the sound and letting the cool liquid slip through my fingertips.

I was so mesmerized by the water falling from this fountain that it took me five minutes to turn around and realize that there actually *was* something waiting there for me.

Behind me there was a small clearing of grass with a statue of God standing in the center against an ivy wall, depicted as in standard Western religions. Sunlight was streaming down onto the statue. Across the clearing—facing the statue—was a stone kneeling bench, so old that half of the stone was turning green with age.

Sitting on top of the kneeler was a single fresh red rose, tied with a red ribbon.

Now I know what most people are going to say. A rose in a cemetery is not uncommon. Let me tell you why this rose was so significant to me.

With everything going on in my life at the time, I was starting to uncover more and more memories of growing up with my mom, taking the time to remember my life in the Before.

This is something about grief that was hard to come to terms with. In the beginning the pain was unbearable. All the memories of my mom were right next to me, weighing on my shoulders, reminding me of everything I had lost.

Then, eventually, they started to fade. Because that was the past, and I was permanently stuck in the present. So as time flew by, moments spent with my mom would often drift away from my mind, and then resurface in my memory at random times.

In this resurfacing, came a smaller, duller sort of pain. The pain of realizing that I was now living a life completely separate from the life that she knew. Things that used to be my daily reality were now just the past. I was in a new normal, and my new normal was *one she would never be in*.

It hurt to remember that I was starting to forget. It hurt to know that Mom was no longer around to remind me.

But suddenly Mom *was* around. At least her energy was. I began to uncover all the memories that had faded away over time.

A few days before coming to this church, I had remembered that voicemail my mom had left, the one I listened to in the hospital the day we realized that she really might not make it out of there alive. And I remembered how—just like in that voicemail—she used to always call me Heather Rosie, because my middle name is Rose.

I stared at the rose lying on the stone. Perfectly wrapped red petals, tied with a little red bow. It was clearly just picked. Its newness was a stark contrast to the garden surrounding, which seemed as if it had sat undisturbed for centuries.

I could practically hear my mom's voice drifting through the wind.

Heather Rosie, Heather Rosie.

Tears welled up in my eyes. I had not used a kneeler since my religious upbringing, but when I saw that rose, I immediately got down on my knees and began speaking to my mom.

"Hey Mom … I'm still trying to figure out what all of this means. But all that I know is that I have never felt your presence more than I do right now. I miss you so much—"

My voice broke. I took a deep breath, then continued.

"I really, really hope that I'm making you proud."

After a few minutes, I wiped a few stray tears from the corners of my eyes. Then I slowly got up and dusted off my knees. I looked down at the kneeler to see an inscription in the stone.

LET NOT YOUR HEART BE TROUBLED

Eventually I left that little garden, a place separate from time.

I got back to my car and pulled out the Forest Lawn map I had been given at the entrance.

I spent the next hour or two walking through mausoleums and various gardens. Intricate marble statues were placed at every turn. It was like I was in a trance. I would pass tombstones, and instead of feeling the crushing weight of death, I felt the power of my ancestors, the wisdom of those that came before me.

It did feel a little insane to me to make this trip to Los Angeles, just to be called to spend the whole day in a cemetery. But it felt right for some reason. I mean it is called the City of Angels.

I eventually found myself drawn to another place on the map.

The Gardens of Remembrance.

I drove down the road and pulled my car off to the side in front of a giant stone mural. On either side of the mural were steps leading up to two platforms. The platforms were covered in grass, and the resting place of loved ones buried. Following the stone path through the tombstones led to another staircase, which led to another platform. And so on. I spent a little time following the stone paths through the various levels of this garden.

Eventually, I found my way under a tree and began to meditate. The rest of the world fell away. I closed my eyes and saw intricate patterns, images, hieroglyphics. I saw the red rose and my mom's smile. I felt connected to Mom now more than ever.

Then I started to cry, overcome with grief again. Not for the mom that I had lost, but for the mom I had still yet to know. I still had so many questions I wished I could ask her. So many things left to say. Especially now, when everything I thought I knew about my world was crumbling.

What do I do now? Where do I go from here?

I wasn't sure, but what I did know now was that Mom *is* the sunshine. I stepped out from under the tree and a warm yellow glow hit my face.

I smiled. *I feel her.*

Eventually I began to follow the stone path back through the many garden platforms, leading me back to my car. As I was walking, one of the many marble sculptures caught my eye, and I walked up to it. Intricately carved was the head of a motherly figure with wavy hair, lovingly looking over her newborn child. Below was an inscription. It was starting to become rusted with age, but as I leaned closer to get a better look, I could just make out the words.

THE ROSE RETURNS TO BLOOM

QUEEN LUCY

> She stayed behind because she thought it would be
> worth while trying the door of the wardrobe, even
> though she felt almost sure that it would be locked.
> To her surprise it opened quite easily …
> —C.S. Lewis, *The Lion, the Witch
> and the Wardrobe*

Earlier that same day, I was standing outside the main mausoleum at Forest Lawn Memorial Park. There were multiple gorgeous white statues surrounding the entrance. I spent some time marveling at each of them.

There was one statue off to the side of the entrance. It was in its own little enclosed area. I approached it and pushed open the small iron gate. As I did, hundreds of little cobweb strings broke open. It was clear that no one had stood in front of this statue in a long time.

I looked up at the statue. It depicted a young woman, standing tall and empowered. She had shoulder length wavy hair and a powerful gaze. In her hands, she held a cloth that draped around her pelvis. The front of the cloth was adorned with flowers.

I stared into the eyes of this statue for a few minutes. It was hard to look away. Just her presence demanded respect. She was soft but strong, emanating grace but also power, appearing gentle but magnetic.

She reminded me of me. Okay, not *me* necessarily, but the me

I *wanted* to be. The me I would be if I was confident, if I learned to stand tall.

After a few minutes, I left the small enclosure and closed the little gate behind me. I felt like I had been standing in a powerful energy field. I felt that energy leave me as I walked away.

After exploring the *Gardens of Remembrance*, I saw the *Gardens of Memory* on the map. I felt called to go there as well, however when I walked up, this place was different from all the other gardens. I wasn't staring at an open curated space, but rather at an old stone wall, inset with a very ancient looking door.

It was about ten feet tall, originally black, but time had begun to stain it green. At the top it said *Gardens of Memory* in gold lettering. To the left of the door was a small sign stating that access to this particular garden was reserved only for beneficiaries and descendants of those that lay in said garden. These were the keepers of the golden keys—keys which would open the door.

I was a bit bummed. I felt drawn to the name. *Gardens of Memory.* I felt like being there was going to be activating somehow.

Try the door anyway.

I closed my hand around the knob and pushed forward.

The door opened. It was ajar.

Suddenly, I was Lucy, stepping through the wardrobe into Narnia. I immediately entered a secret paradise. A few hundred feet of lush green grass lay in front of me. Inset into the ground were hundreds of grass markers. Around the edge of the green ivy walls were various other statues and mausoleums. There were side staircases leading up to smaller gardens. One even led to an open-air room, the *Columbarium of Sunlight.*

I spent a long time exploring this secret garden, another moment away from time.

But the reason I tell this story is not because of the magnificence of the space. It is because of the first thing I saw, the very first thing I locked eyes with, the second the magic door opened.

It was *her*.

The powerful young marble woman I had been magnetized by a few hours earlier. Here she was *again* in this garden. And if I was drawn to her before, now it was tenfold.

She was higher this time, elevated on a marble podium maybe five or six feet into the air, overlooking a mausoleum. Her stone flowers were now complemented by real white and purple ones on either side. The green ivy wall made a stark backdrop to her ghost-white figure, and the sunlight cast a heavenly glow directly onto her form.

I found myself staring at her again for a long time. My chin raised and looking up this time, for she had ascended higher.

When I eventually left that magical secret garden, I just kept thinking to myself, *that* is who I want to be.

That is who I could be, if I stopped letting myself and others hold me back.

That is who I was born to be, who I could become.

I didn't understand why I was so drawn to this statue when I saw her the first time, but in that moment, I realized.

I had caught a glimpse of my Higher Self.

METAMORPHOSIS

I almost wish I hadn't gone down that rabbit
hole—and yet—and yet—it's rather curious, you
know, this sort of life! … I used to read fairy tales,
I fancied that kind of thing never happened, and
now here I am in the middle of one! There ought
to be a book written about me, that there ought!
And when I grow up, I'll write one …
—Lewis Carroll, *Alice's Adventures
in Wonderland*

I decided I wanted to make a vision board. I had never done it before, but it seemed fitting, as I was leaving my job and basically starting my life from scratch. I asked Morgan to join me, so we had a tentative plan to make them together at some point soon.

The next day I was scrolling through my local Buy Nothing Facebook group. I had been on there a lot recently, since I had just moved into my new apartment and needed a lot of supplies.

My jaw dropped as I read the caption on the most recent post:

Speed Gifting
Does anyone want these magazines for a vision board project or something of the sort? They've been sitting outside in the sun. I'll be tossing them tonight before they get soaked from the rain.

Below the caption was a picture of a giant pile of magazines.

I laughed. Here I was, just talking about making a vision board with my friend, and there was this post. *Do you want to make a vision board? Here are supplies!*

The woman lived at an apartment about three blocks away, so I messaged her that I was on my way, and started walking. As I approached a corner, I looked over to the right and saw a pole with a flier.

Crazy Greg's Yard Sale
August Sat 19
One day only! Don't sleep on this one!

The sale was happening right at that moment. I figured I would head over there after getting these magazines.

I crossed the street and continued walking. About a minute later, my phone buzzed in my pocket. It was a message from the Facebook woman. She was so sorry, but she accidentally got one of the numbers wrong on the address she sent me. She texted the correct address, and it was about a block and a half back the way I came—I had walked too far.

I turned around and started making my way back, but I could feel an energy rising within me. I began to tense with frustration.

I walked over there for nothing! Time wasted …

I stopped myself before I got further into this negative thought spiral. Had I learned *anything* from the power of slowing down and paying attention? If I just walked an extra block down the street, *it must've been for a reason.*

Realization dawned on me as I remembered the garage sale flier I had snapped a picture of only five minutes ago. I forgot where exactly I had seen it. I pulled out my phone, went to the photo, and looked at the geotag underneath.

Sure enough, it was posted on the farther cross street. Which means that if the woman had given me her correct address, if I hadn't walked those extra few minutes, *I wouldn't have seen it.*

That means you have to go there. There's something you need to find there.

Maybe the voice was crazy, and it was just a coincidence. But nevertheless, this garage sale might have a good pot I could buy. So after I picked up my magic magazines gifted to me from the universe, I set off toward this garage sale.

A few minutes later, I approached a house with a small sign pointing toward a path.

Garage sale this way!

I walked down the narrow path to the back of the house. There were a few tables set up, covered with random items, but the first thing that caught my eye was the sign that was posted above them. I stared at the words in disbelief.

Prices too crazy?? Let's make a deal!

Below it was a printed screenshot of their Venmo QR code.

To give you a sense of the timeline here, I had filmed my episode of *Let's Make a Deal* in Los Angeles *three days before this.*

Three days before this, I was standing on a soundstage and filming a game show, all because a crazy opportunity was presented to me while on the way to a garage sale a few weeks ago. Now, here I was at a different garage sale, with a sign denoting the name of that very show.

See, you are meant to be here. This isn't a coincidence.

I took a few minutes to look around at the various tables, but nothing caught my eye. It was mostly random junk and old clothes. So I went over to the book section—my favorite part of any garage sale. I love seeing what kinds of stories I can find.

I scanned the titles and read the backs of covers, ending my search with a pile of four books that drew me in.

One of them called out to me. Illustrated on the cover was a blue sky filled with clouds. *Skyfaring* by Mark Vanhoenacker. A book written by a pilot about the magic and miracle that truly is plane travel.

Whenever I am on a plane, I always take the window seat. I find myself, jaw open, eyes wide, staring out at the beauty and magic of the earth before me. I take hundreds of pictures of the clouds on my phone. I simply cannot get over the view. No matter how many flights I go on, the wonderment that washes over me is always the same. But then I look around at the other passengers on the plane, the people sitting, watching their movies, scrolling on their iPhones. I can feel the watching eyes of the people sitting next to me, the sense of judgment, the thoughts of, *Hmm this must be her first time on a plane.*

It always baffles me. I don't understand how anyone could sit on a plane, soaring above the clouds, and not marvel at the beauty of the universe. I find myself thinking about that often, how many beautiful things in this world we've stopped looking at, stopped appreciating, because we've experienced them before. It's no longer novel to us.

Yeah, I've seen the clouds before. I've seen the wisps of white flow through the air, the clouds as fluffy as a cotton ball, looking like I could jump down onto them like a trampoline. I've seen the sunrise appear on the horizon as we zoom through the air and chase the rest of the day's light. I've seen the vast expanse of rivers, mountains, and deserts that make the most interesting and intricate patterns when looked at from above. I've seen it all before.

And I hope I get to see it a million times more.

So I felt a sense of kinship with this pilot author. Someone who has probably been on hundreds of flights, and yet did not let the repetition of his job cloud him to the true magic of what he gets to experience on a regular basis.

I paid for this book, and three others, and started walking back to my apartment.

As I made my way home, my arms full of magazines and books, I looked down at the ground and saw a blue Styrofoam butterfly, about six inches tall, laying on the sidewalk.

I smiled. Lately I had been thinking a lot about butterflies and what they symbolize.

Rebirth. Transformation.

That was me. I turned the key in the lock and walked back into my own cocoon, setting the large stack of magazines and books on the counter.

As I struggled to place them down, some of the books slid off the magazines and onto the ground. I noticed something slip out of the *Skyfaring* book. It was a card.

I bent down to pick the card off the floor and flipped it over. The cover was purple, adorned with Monarch butterflies.

Wow, I thought to myself. There actually *was* something for me to find at the garage sale! This lovely butterfly card, reminding me of the transformation I was undergoing. The purple made me think it was Mom that sent it. I felt a sense of warmth enter my heart.

I flipped the card open and was surprised to discover that it wasn't empty. It was full of scribbles, inscriptions written from multiple people to Greg, the man from the garage sale.

I stilled—the way you do when standing in your house, suddenly overcome by the feeling that you may not be alone.

I couldn't believe what I was reading. This butterfly card was a *goodbye* card to Greg.

From his *coworkers*.

He was leaving his job, and so they were sending him off with warm sentiments and support. One note really caught my attention:

Greg, congratulations on nearing the end / beginning.
I know you'll get a good job soon.

At the time I read those words, I was only *three days away* from my last day at my news job. I had no plan, and doubt was starting to creep in.

But this card reaffirmed my faith. I wasn't crazy. There were larger forces at play here. I had my mom and my angels on my side.

This was only the beginning.

HEAD IN THE CLOUDS

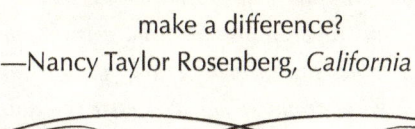

> She was everything they said she was—
> a loony, a goofball, a dreamer. How could
> an intelligent, rational mind tender such
> ridiculous thoughts? How could she possibly
> think that she alone could ever
> make a difference?
> —Nancy Taylor Rosenberg, *California Angel*

I woke up one morning and it was the last day of my job.

I felt fine for the better part of the morning. I went to my assignments and filmed events as usual. But as the hours ticked closer and closer toward the end of my shift, I started to feel a change in my energy.

The overwhelming sense of finality hit as I unpacked my company backpack and brought my equipment back to my supervisor's office. It wasn't that long ago that I was filling that backpack on my very first day, printing out little name labels to stick on my camera and tripod.

I wanted to keep my emotions in check, but as I began to speak to my supervisor for the last time, I could feel my face flushing and the tears starting to come in—I had gone through many endings in my short time here on earth, but it still hadn't made them any easier.

As soon as I began to thank him for his guidance during my time at the station, unsanctioned tears started flowing. I wiped them away from the corner of my eye.

"I'm not good with endings," I explained.

"It's not an ending," he replied. "It's just a new beginning."

I rushed to my car and shut the door behind me. Then came the waterworks. I sobbed and sobbed. I drove past the company building and out through the gate, acutely aware that it was my very last time driving through it. I used my shirt to wipe the emotion from my face as the doubt started to creep in.

What are you doing? What if this was all a big mistake? What are you going to do now? You quit your job without a backup plan? You're going to drain your bank account and fail. You want to make your own money? You're not capable. You can't do it. You just lost your golden opportunity. Everyone was so proud of you. What are you doing?

I cried the whole way home. One of those loud, guttural cries.

As much as I had faith in my decision to leave, saying you are going to leave and actually *doing it* are two very different things. I thought of my sister who told me she thought I was making a mistake. I thought of my uncle who said he was proud of me for getting this ABC job. What would he think when he found out I threw it all away?

Was everyone about to watch my downfall?

Confronted with the ramifications of my actions and the overwhelming weight of the unknown, I shrunk into myself. I felt like a scared little girl, alone in the world.

I closed the door to my apartment and collapsed into my chair. Tears blurred my vision as I turned to see the quote book I had sitting on my desk.

The Most Important Thing I've Learned in Life: 370 Lessons to Live By, edited and compiled by Beau Bauman. In a moment of desperation, I picked it up and fingered its pages.

I had recently purchased this book from a garage sale and started to use it like an oracle, flipping the book open to a random page and seeing what guidance it had to share with me on a given day.

It was working too—so well that I brought it to work a week ago, just for fun. I had the reporter I was paired with flip open to a page after we had just dealt with a stressful situation involving miscommunication with the producers. The quote she opened it up to?

"To hate incompetence."

—*Ben Foti, chief videotape editor*
Fox 5
New York

A freaking Fox 5 employee? I had just been using the book as a fun motivator, but on that day, I began to actually believe in its abilities.

And if there was any day that I needed some words of wisdom, it was that day. I felt myself becoming paralyzed with fear. I was desperate for some guidance, some nugget of motivation.

I closed my eyes and flipped the book open. My sobs became harder, my vision blurrier, but a smile slowly crossed my face as I read the words:

"The ultimate defense against growing old is your dream. Nothing is as real as a dream. Your dream is the path between the person you are and the person you hope to become. Success isn't money. Success isn't power. The criteria for your success are to be found in your dream, in your self. Your dream is something to hold on to. It will always be your link with the person you are today, young and full of hope. If you hold on to it, you may grow old, but you will never be old. And that is the ultimate success."

—*Tom Clancy, author*
New York

My body shook in a paradoxical combination of grief and laughter. At this point I shouldn't have been surprised that the universe was here offering their support, but honestly it still feels magical every time.

My mystical quote book reminded me of the reason I took this leap of faith in the first place. I knew the road ahead might be difficult and bumpy and full of unknowns, but I was going to keep pushing. I was no longer willing to sacrifice my dreams for anything. Not for money, not for other people, not for acceptance, not for stability.

My dreams are what keep me moving forward.

For too long, I had been standing still.

SILENCE

"You're not a lotus-eater, Mona," Nigel said patiently. "Not anymore. You're back on the boat, heading home. It's time you sat orderly upon the bench and smote the gray sea with your oars. Row hard and don't look back."
—Jen Beagin, *Pretend I'm Dead*

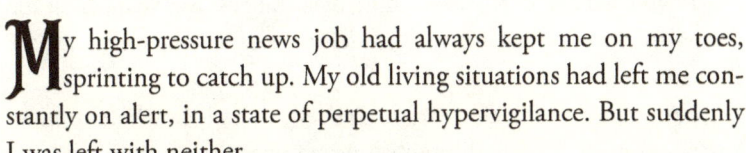

My high-pressure news job had always kept me on my toes, sprinting to catch up. My old living situations had left me constantly on alert, in a state of perpetual hypervigilance. But suddenly I was left with neither.

I woke up the next morning, and it was just … quiet.

The next month was a month of silence.

I was now unemployed and living fully alone for the first time. On top of that, my extreme burnout from my job was making me quite the antisocial hermit. Being around others had become too draining.

I was also catapulted out of my old coping mechanisms. I did not bring a TV to this new apartment, so I just stopped watching television. I threw out my dab pen, and I poured the last bottle of wine I had down the drain.

As much work as I had done on my self-concept up to this point, this was the time when the work really began. You might say you love yourself, but how would it feel to be alone with your mind for a full day without distraction, without talking to another human being? How would it feel to be in your mind alone for days on end?

There was a crushing loneliness I had felt when my mom left this earth, and now it was tenfold. I had no family, no coworkers, no friends I could turn to to numb the void. Even if I were to call my sisters, they wouldn't understand what I was going through. My phone sat on the table untouched.

I used to do anything to escape sitting with my own thoughts. My mind was a terrible and scary place I did not want to be in. I would distract myself in any way possible. But now the distractions didn't work. Because I *knew* they were distractions.

You know the saying, ignorance is bliss?

Well, I was no longer ignorant and no longer blissful. I *knew* I was running from myself. So I no longer found joy in the drinking and the smoking and the doom scrolling—only more shame.

I had tried absolutely everything over the past five years to escape the pain. Nothing had worked. I couldn't escape. The only way out was through.

When you sit in silence with yourself, there is nowhere to hide. You're confronted with all the feelings you have spent your life running from. A lot of memories came bubbling up to the surface.

If the idea of sitting with your own mind for that long sounds unbearable to you, I can tell you that that's a marker of how desperately you *need* the silence.

Because I've come to learn that *the things we resist the most, are actually the things that will provide us with the most growth and change in ourselves.*

As the famous saying by Dipen Parmar goes, "The magic you are looking for is in the work you are avoiding."

It was time to stop running away. Time to face and fully accept all parts of myself. Time to go deeper.

FRESH EYES

You spend your whole life stuck in the
labyrinth, thinking about how you'll escape
it one day, and how awesome it will be,
and imagining that future keeps you going,
but you never do it. You just use the future
to escape the present.
—John Green, *Looking for Alaska*

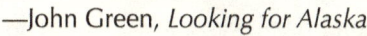
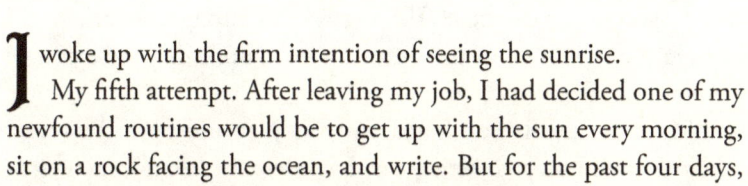

I woke up with the firm intention of seeing the sunrise.

My fifth attempt. After leaving my job, I had decided one of my newfound routines would be to get up with the sun every morning, sit on a rock facing the ocean, and write. But for the past four days, I'd been filling blank pages under gloomy clouds.

As I got dressed, I peeked through my windows and saw gray clouds. I figured this might be yet another vain attempt, but I pulled on my shoes anyway. I was resolved to go write—whether or not the sun decided to join me.

When I stepped outside and my eyes adjusted, it was not the gray overcast morning I had grown accustomed to. Instead, a thick, milky fog covered the streets like an omniscient shadow. I could not see more than fifty feet in front of me.

I looked around for a moment, in awe. Then I began walking.

In the distance, two pinpricks of light appeared in the gray. The hazy yellow glow got stronger and stronger, until a car jolted its way out of the unknown and sped past me. The street corners I passed daily were now popping into view with a new unfamiliarity. I looked up at the palm trees. With each row that stretched back, the palms became hazier—more and more of a distant memory.

I came upon a small spider web tucked into a bush on the side of a blue house. The lines of silk connected in mesmerizingly intricate geometric patterns, and each thread was beaded with small pearls of dew—so small and so delicate, it appeared as though it was nature's finest work of art. I examined each drop with wonder, taking a picture in my mind. I ambled on.

It wasn't long before the sidewalk paralleled along the shoreline. One or two shadowy figures could be seen standing out in the sand, but anything beyond them was a mystery. The fog had completely enveloped the ocean. No water to be seen.

I wondered if it had ever existed.

I continued along the sidewalk and the pier came into view. I had forgotten it was there! The fog was so strong that one could not grasp any inkling of the pier's existence until they were a mere hundred feet from its threshold.

My path usually continued past the pier and onto the rocks, where I would stop to write, but I was enraptured by this fog. I wanted to be *in* it. I wanted to be enveloped by the unknown. So I climbed the steps to the pier and continued my journey.

I stepped forward along the concrete and looked at the expanse of gray before me. A formidable wall of mist. Suddenly, a bicyclist materialized and whizzed past me. I turned around. A futile attempt—he was already a memory. It was just me on this pier, with small patches of ocean rippling on either side.

Beyond that, only gray.

I floated along, looking with newfound wonder at the things I *could* see. The things right in front of me. I looked to my left and seven birds emerged and flew past in a V. They were gone as swiftly as they had come.

A group of people came into view. They were fishing. I walked past the handful of them with their fishing lines in hand and buckets on the ground. It was as if I had happened upon a hidden, ancient village. I locked eyes with the last woman in the collective, and then I trekked on.

I stepped over to the edge of the pier and looked out at the world. An expanse of ocean was before me, a stretch of beach, numerous buildings—a whole civilization I had just ventured from and would soon return to, and yet I could see none of it. Just my fifty feet of ocean, and this gray mist.

Did that make those things any less real?

This must be what faith feels like.

I kept walking. I wanted to get to the very end of the pier—*isn't that what one does when walking on piers?*

But why? I was not quite sure, because I soon realized that its view was the same as all the other views I had collected along my journey: a small stretch of ocean, and then emptiness.

In the past few weeks, I had been reflecting on my life and I realized that I had not been living it. Every moment my body was present, my mind was off in a different time and space. It was focused on the future, on documenting, on getting somewhere, on what I would do next, on where I was supposed to be instead. Or, it was clouded by the past, by my trauma, by my limiting beliefs, by my incessant inner critic telling me that I was not good enough and I never would be.

I had made a commitment to myself that in this next chapter of my life, no matter what happened, no matter what I still wanted or what goals I was working toward, I would learn to ground myself and live in the present moment.

But how *difficult* it is to live a life of meaning and intention in a world so obsessed with the commodification of time. It was so ingrained into me that even though I had left my job in order to heal, I found myself having to beg my mind just to let me rest, to enjoy, to *live* without feeling guilty.

Yet, here on this morning, the fog descended, *forcing* me to stay in the present and only look a few steps ahead. I couldn't help but laugh. The universe is nothing if not clever.

I was grateful for the lesson.

As I sat on the pier and etched my last few words onto paper, I reached up a hand to wipe my face. I felt a wetness as I realized my eyelashes were glazed in dew. I smiled, and said a little prayer of thanks to the fog, for allowing me to see my world with Fresh Eyes.

NOAH'S ARK

And where most people see mirrors, you, my
friend, see windows. By which I mean there is
always something beyond the glass. You have
seen it and will always see it now, though others
may not. I would have spared you that vision
at such a young age. But it's been given you,
and it will be up to you to decide whether
it's a blessing or a curse.
—Trenton Lee Stewart, *The Mysterious
Benedict Society and the Perilous Journey*

As much as I had told myself, *Heather, you can afford to take a
month to heal from your burnout before you start looking for a job
to help support you while pursuing your business goals,* soon enough in
the silence, I found myself stressing, panicking, and wondering why
the *fuck* I left my job with no plan.

Was I crazy?

Deep down I knew I wasn't crazy. My burnout was so bad that
I didn't have any other options. But we're so programmed to believe
that we have to work, work, *work,* that I couldn't let my brain rest
the way I knew it needed to. Within a week, I started desperately
searching for lucrative digital skills I could learn, or remote jobs that
aligned with my current skill set. I spent my days scrolling through
Tik Tok, learning about profitable freelance ventures like copywriting

and remote closing.

The thing is, I'm intelligent and I pick up skills quickly, so I *knew* if I pursued something like this, I would be "successful." But I couldn't. I couldn't write copy for just any business to market their products.

My soul would not let me do it.

I *needed* to feel like I was making a difference somehow, or I would slowly feel like I was wasting away. That's how I felt in my prior job, because there was a lot about the broadcast news industry that didn't sit right with me ethically. I could no longer compromise my morals for money.

Eventually, I found a marketing position with a nonprofit that had a mission I believed in. *This is it*, my voice of rationality thought. Maybe nonprofits were my ticket to making income without feeling like a sellout. *Maybe the spiritual coaching thing is just a potential side hobby.*

I submitted an application.

A day or two later, I was scrolling through Tik Tok, and a video appeared. It was Kenzie Swaine again. The angel girl.

This time, she was saying that if you need immediate help from your angels, you could ask them if you are on the right or wrong path and give them a twenty-four hour limit to get your answer.

Even with all the crazy things that had been happening in my life lately, I was a bit skeptical with this time limit request with my angels. I didn't want to be pushy. Would they be able to deliver?

But again, *what did I have to lose?*

I looked up at the ceiling.

"Angels, I think this nonprofit job might be the opportunity I've been waiting for. Is this the right path for me?"

I thought to myself for a moment.

"If it is, in twenty-four hours show me a narwhal. And if it isn't, show me a skunk."

Later that night, I was at Morgan's apartment. We were going to make our vision boards with my stack of magical magazines. I hadn't opened them yet; I wanted it to be a surprise. I showed up on her doorstep with the stack under one arm and a cork board under the other.

I had never created a vision board before. To be honest, I didn't even know what I wanted to put on it when I showed up that night. I knew people often put images of the car they want, or the house. I knew that wasn't what I cared about.

Then I opened these magazines.

We began flipping through the pages, and it became immediately clear to me just how divine it was that they had crossed my path. I was staring at so many quotes, snippets, stories, putting onto paper everything I dreamed of creating, but hadn't had the words to verbalize yet. I found myself cutting out endless words and quotes, coming face to face with my vision.

My plain brown corkboard started coming to life. With every piece of tape, I began crafting the narrative of my dreams. A life where I create an impact, one that really helps people, beyond just profit. A life where I share my stories and my knowledge, creating a community on social media—not for fame or affluence, but to give people permission to be seen and share in the same way. A life where my focus is always about spreading love and acceptance. A life where I learn how to speak and use my voice to stand in my truth. A life built with intention. A life where I have influence, and I use it for good.

At the beginning of this book, I told you that when I tried to envision my life in the future, I drew a blank. I never fully believed that the future was a place in which I would exist.

Staring at the words on this board, I could *see* it. I could *see* this future. It didn't matter how far I was from it. What mattered was that I *finally* saw a reality that I believed I could exist in.

At the center of my board was the title, *Life by Design*.

It seemed fitting. I was burning my old life to the ground to create my new one, brick by brick.

Below this title was a full-page quote I found by Rumi in one of the magazines. It created the focal point of my board:

"Keep walking, though there's no place to get to.
Don't try to see through the distances.
That's not for human beings. Move within,
But don't move the way fear makes you move.

If you are irritated by every rub, how will your
mirror be polished?

Start a huge, foolish project like Noah … it makes
absolutely no difference what people think of you."

At the end of that night, staring at all those powerful words, I felt myself getting increasingly excited at the possibilities of what I could create.

Soon it was getting dark, and Morgan walked with me down the street to my car. Right as I was about to open the door, she spoke.

"Hmm, do you smell that? It smells like a skunk."

My heart dropped into my chest. I had almost forgotten about my challenge with the angels.

A skunk? *Fuck.*

The wrong path.

Back to square one.

The next day I woke up uneasy. *The wrong path?* I thought I had been following my angels' guidance.

Was this all a mistake? Was it all in my head?

But then I looked over at my vision board.

Start a huge, foolish project like Noah.

The skunk began to make more sense to me. Dreams don't just appear out of thin air. They are planted in our hearts for a reason. If everything on that board was what I was supposed to create in this lifetime, why would I waste my time taking an entry-level position at a nonprofit?

You aren't meant to be a cog in a machine. You are meant to build a whole new one.

I laughed. The voice was right. I'm nothing if not unconventional.

But what would I do now? I was staring at a board full of dreams. None of it was in my physical reality. I didn't know how to bridge the gap.

Keep walking. Don't try to see through the distances. Move within.

I found myself reflecting on all the lessons I had begun to learn that month, about living in the present moment, surrendering to life's circumstances, and not planning and stressing about every little thing. I had seen firsthand that *living by these lessons is where the magic gets created.*

But the stress of making money had overtaken me and washed away all those lessons. I was trying to take control of my life again, instead of giving the universe the reins.

Not only that, but I was still extremely burnt out. That was the reason I left my job in the first place. I needed to rest. I needed to heal. I needed to find the joy in life again. I needed to fill my own cup. I couldn't accomplish anything on that vision board if I was still broken.

So over the next few days, I reset. I put the idea of money on the backburner, and I once again tried to prioritize building myself back up. I committed to my morning routine and my journaling practice. I went on adventures that brought me joy, I tried new things, and most importantly, I reprioritized meditation, like the psychic had told me to. I knew that that was the most important way to reclaim my peace.

I felt my mental clarity returning, and soon the idea of asking my angels if I was on the right track came back to me.

I wanted to try again. I felt like I had found a better path, even though it provided me with no concrete answers for my future.

It had also occurred to the practical part of my brain, that maybe it was just a *coincidence* that my friend mentioned a skunk that night.

Maybe a skunk was too easy. And maybe it was completely insane and irrational to plan my entire life around that experience. So at the very least, I wanted to try the angel practice again with more difficult symbols in order to gain empirical evidence.

And to decide if I was absolutely crazy.

Time to look up to the sky again.

"Okay Angels, the past few days I've been surrendering more, taking time to heal, to observe, and to prioritize my meditation, instead of focusing on money and a 'responsible' plan. Is *that* what you want me to do? If yes, show me a trident. And if not, show me a cheetah."

I paused for a moment, and then added, "Also, you can't show me Trident gum. That's a copout. I need the full Poseidon symbol."

It was morning when I asked this. Throughout the rest of the day, I walked around town on high alert, looking over my shoulder and checking stickers on car windows I passed.

I was desperate for my answer. I was desperate to know that I wasn't crazy.

But I saw nothing. Eventually I forgot about it.

The day I asked for this sign was August 31st, 2023.

That night, there was going to be a blue supermoon—a rare celestial event that only occurs every ten years or so. There were videos on my Tik Tok feed about harnessing the power of this rare astrological event, and about it being the best time to set intentions and release what wasn't serving me.

I usually was not one to pay attention to these things, but I'd also been hesitantly communicating with my angels for the past month.

Starting to believe in the power of astrology was not *that* much of a stretch. I thought doing a blue supermoon ritual could be fun. So Morgan and I made plans to do just that.

She came over to my apartment that night. The plan was to walk over to the beach and journal under the moon.

I grabbed a towel, a notebook, and a pen. As we were about to walk out the door, Morgan asked, "Wait, how will we be able to see in the dark to be able to journal?"

She had a point. My gaze wandered, and then landed on my Guardian Angel candle from the mini mart. I had been lighting it almost daily—it seemed fitting. I grabbed the candle and my blue lighter, and then we set out for the ocean.

We made it to the shore, and I laid my green towel out over the sand. I lit the Guardian Angel candle and placed it on the towel, slowly pushing it down into the sand to secure it. Then we pulled out our journals and began writing.

After a few minutes, the candle fell over. Smooth, white wax spilled onto the towel and solidified.

"Oh no, that's so annoying!" I exclaimed.

"That's okay, I'm sure it will wash out," Morgan replied.

I laughed. I was still learning how to not let my moods be dictated by external circumstances. Morgan was right; it wasn't that serious. It was just a towel, and washing machines exist. Nothing to do about it *now*. No reason to let it interrupt our time.

So instead of trying to clean it up, I ignored it and went back to our journal ritual—we were writing about everything we wanted to release in order to step into a better version of ourselves.

I had a lot to release—my tendency to let other people and circumstances influence my emotions ... my fear of failure ... my fear of being successful ... my feeling that I am unworthy of what I want, of success, of attention ... my belief that I am incapable of the things I want to pursue ... my worry about other people's opinions that keeps me from standing in my power as my true authentic self ... the painful memories holding me back.

After I finished my list, I ripped my page out of the journal and walked toward the shoreline. I read the words out loud three times, my voice drowned out by the booming crash of the waves in front of me.

"I release … I release … I release …"

The longer I spoke, the more powerful my tone became, and the more I could feel myself letting go of the parts of me that no longer served the Me I wanted to become.

I finished the last sentence and returned to the towel. Morgan and I dug a hole in the sand and stuck our pages inside. Then I grabbed my lighter and we set fire to our burdens.

We watched as the orange and blue flames slowly crept over the edges of the paper, leaving black singed marks in their wake. Eventually the fire grew, the flame wisping up into the air a few inches, engulfing the pages as they slowly shrank and shrank further into themselves, contorting into a new form.

Soon, there was almost no white visible. The paper continued folding into itself, creating a new shape. Morgan and I watched, entranced, as the blackened chrysalis slowly shrunk into the shape of a heart. An orange glow traced over the final burn lines of this heart, illuminating it one last time, before the fire died and we were left with a pile of ash.

"Woah," Morgan said. "Did you see that?"

"Yeah. That was crazy," I replied softly.

About twenty minutes later, we were back in my apartment, and Morgan was about to head home. My bag was lying on the floor with my green towel sitting next to it.

We hugged goodbye and talked about when we would see each other next. As we spoke, I saw Morgan's gaze move beyond my eyes and focus on something behind me.

"Hey, that wax on your towel kind of looks like a chicken foot!

With the three prongs," she remarked.

My heart leaped in my chest.

Three prongs?

I had completely forgotten about the test I had set up for my angels earlier that day—I had asked for a trident.

But there's absolutely no way, right? Like, that's not possible. There's no way there's a trident sitting on my towel right now.

I slowly turned around, walked across the room, and knelt by the towel.

In the corner was an expanse of white, milky candle wax. But within the wax was a shape. Somehow this part of the wax had become darker, blackened. It looked different than the rest of the wax. It looked like a brand.

And this brand took the form of one line, a line that forked up into three distinct prongs.

A trident.

Okay Angels, I believe. I'll meditate. I'll do what you tell me. Show me the way.

The Boy with the Hat

"I advise you to sail away in one of your
ships, and never come home again 'till
you have tried your own way," said Jo,
whose imagination was fired by the
thought of such a daring exploit …
—Louisa May Alcott, *Little Women*

I walked along the shoreline with my backpack strung over my
shoulder. It was full of books, my journal, and a towel. I was
planning to go sit along the rocks of Sunset Cliffs.

It was daytime, and the sidewalk was full of people enjoying the
view and the warm salty air—a *lot* of people. I once again practiced
straightening my spine and raising my head tall as I strode past wandering eyes.

As I walked past the steps that led up the pier, I noticed a man
sitting on the stone outcropping, overlooking the water. His warm
honey skin glowed in the sunlight and a cowboy hat cast a light
shadow over his face. There was nothing that made him stand out
from any of the dozens of other people on the sidewalk.

Tell him you like his hat.

My step faltered—I was already about to walk right past him.
I had a split second to react to the voice in my head, and in that
second, I decided it wasn't necessary. I wasn't going to stop and turn
around just to tell this guy he had a cool hat. I didn't want him to

think I was trying to hit on him.

I kept walking and found a promising rock to settle on. I laid out my towel over the rough stone and wrote in my journal for an hour or so. Then I closed my eyes and began to meditate.

A little while later, I raised my eyelids to let the daylight back in, getting reacquainted with reality. As I blinked a few times, I noticed there was someone standing a few feet in front of me on the rock, his back to me, staring out at the ocean waves.

It was the boy with the hat.

Well hat-boy was right in front of me now. I had to say something.

"Hey, I just wanted to say I like your hat!" I said cheerfully.

"Thank you!" A warm smile lit up the face underneath the hat, and he began to tell me where he got it from.

After a few minutes of talking, he took a few steps closer to me. He asked me if I lived in the area and how I liked San Diego. I told him how I loved living near the ocean. San Diego was great, but especially Ocean Beach, where the two of us were. There was a magical energy about this beach.

He told me that this was his first day—his first *hour*—in San Diego, and I was the first person he had met since arriving.

"No way! You just got here? Where did you come from?" I asked.

Apparently, it wasn't a question with a simple answer. He sat down on the rock edge a few feet from me and explained that he was from New York.

"Me too!" I cut in.

"No way!" he exclaimed.

He continued to tell me how he had started to question living in New York City. "I was always such a straight arrow. Calculating moves. Thinking about the future," he began.

But something changed. He started to feel lost and unfulfilled. Since his engineering job was remote, he booked a trip to Arizona to clear his head. The next thing he knew he was standing in the Arizona airport, bags in hand to return to New York. But something stopped him. He walked up to the flight counter, and instead, booked a one-way ticket to San Diego.

Now he was here on a rock talking to me.

I listened to his story with my mouth open in awe. Imagine walking into the airport, an *entire plan* for your next steps in place, and then just thinking, *Fuck it*, and spontaneously flying in the opposite direction.

It was a level of freedom that I wanted for myself. It was a level of surrender I didn't know if I would ever be able to master.

I traded his spontaneous *fuck-it* story for my own, explaining how I was a photojournalist for *ABC News*, how my family was so proud of me, and how I threw it all away to become a girl sitting on a rock with no clear plan for the future.

Doubt clouded my head every day since I had left. I expressed how lost I felt, how I wondered if I threw everything away.

"Wait, how old are you?" hat-boy interjected.

"Twenty-three," I replied.

"Oh!" he began laughing. "You're only twenty-three? You have your whole life ahead of you to figure things out. If a job burned you out that fast, then it clearly just wasn't for you. Now your days are open to discover what is."

His light-hearted reaction lifted me up. He was right. I *was* only twenty-three.

I think I had fallen so deep into the need to have it all figured out right away, that I had forgotten how young I was. I had forgotten just how many opportunities I still had to learn, and pivot, and walk up to flight counters and decide to go in a completely different direction. Hat-boy was in his thirties. If he could change his plans and rediscover himself, then so could I.

We continued talking. He mentioned in passing that he had lost both his parents. My heart ached. I told him I was sorry for his loss and I understood—I had lost my mom a few years back.

Around this time, I had begun to read the *Signs* book from the garage sale, and I had begun to see signs that my mom was still with me. Part of me thought it would be inappropriate to talk about it with this person I just met, but as we spoke of grief, I was feeling the urge to mention it to him.

"Okay, you might think I'm weird, but …"

I told him about the signs I was getting from my mom on the other side and how much peace it brought me where there used to only be darkness.

He didn't think I was crazy. He hadn't had experiences like that of his own, but he didn't think I was strange. He listened with an open heart and mind. We continued talking about death, life, and choosing what we really want rather than the preset paths that are laid out for us by others.

An hour or so later, I backtracked. "I'm Heather, by the way!" I exclaimed and held out my hand.

"I'm Alex," hat-boy said, chuckling as he shook my hand.

I joined in the laughter. Funny how we could talk about grief and signs from angels before even having a name to put to each other's faces—I guess we needed icebreakers before divulging something *that* serious.

We stayed for about two and a half hours, talking on that rock, only breaking when we realized we were getting horribly burned in the California sun.

Funny, how of all the hats I could've complimented on the beach, I chose the one attached to a boy with such striking similarities to me—from New York and getting a new start in San Diego, feeling the need to switch directions in life, overcoming grief of a parent.

He asked for my number, and I typed his contact into my phone. *Alex with the Hat.*

TRAUMA HEATHER

I'll tell them how I survive it. I'll tell them that
on bad mornings, it feels impossible to take
pleasure in anything because I'm afraid it
could be taken away. That's when I make a list
in my head of every act of goodness I've seen
someone do. It's like a game. Repetitive …
But there are much worse games to play.
—Suzanne Collins, *Mockingjay*

The earliest birthday that I remember is second grade. I was turning eight.

Flowers swayed in the breeze of spring as I skipped down the
sidewalk and into the reddish tan building that was my elementary
school.

I continued to bounce down the hallway toward Mrs. Krill's
second grade classroom. I loved Mrs. Krill. She always made everyone feel extra special on their birthday.

I turned and floated through the door. Then I looked up and
halted in my step.

That isn't Mrs. Krill.

Standing at the front of the classroom was a young man with
curly jet-black hair.

A substitute.

I tried to hide my disappointment as I pulled out my chair and sat at my small coffee-colored desk. Pasted at the top was a nametag, *Heather* scrawled in seven-year-old Sharpie penmanship to the left, and a mini addition table to the right. My eyelids drooped down, staring through the grid of numbers until it became an indistinct blob.

I heard my name and perked my head up. The substitute teacher was beckoning me toward the front of the room where a storage closet sat. He stood with his hands behind his back.

I hesitantly walked over, and once I was standing there, he brought his arms in front of him. Outstretched in his hands was a hot pink plastic bowler hat. A ribbon ran around its center, adorned in confetti and *Happy Birthday* written in neon lettering.

"Mrs. Krill told me that it was your birthday today!" he exclaimed.

A smile lit up my face. I couldn't believe that Mrs. Krill had remembered and told the substitute to celebrate the occasion on her behalf.

I took my little pink hat back to my seat and put it on—me beaming from ear to ear definitely added to the spectacle.

Soon after this, the two girls who sat to my right turned and started talking to me.

They usually didn't do this. They wished me a happy birthday. They were being extra nice.

One of the girls' names was Maria. She had brown, curly hair and olive skin. I cannot remember the other girl's name, but I do remember her face. Caramel skin and black hair.

Maria flipped her thick hair back over her shoulder and pulled a highlighter out of her desk. It was one of the fancy ones we could buy at the school store, shaped in a triangle with a different color on each corner.

She handed it to me. A birthday present, she explained.

The other girl followed suit, pulling a few pencils out of her own desk and passing them to me.

It hadn't occurred to me that suddenly being this nice to me in May, after the *entire* school year had passed, should have been a warning flag.

Since the year was almost over, we were going to have to clean out our desks in a few days. Maria took it upon herself to start doing the work early.

"Wait, I have more!" Maria said a few minutes later.

My pink bowler hat was sitting upside down on my desk at this point. She dropped in a few markers, and a pencil with an eraser on the end shaped like a monkey head. The girl beside her added some more wares.

This continued on for a few minutes. Soon my bowler hat was filled to the brim with random fun pencils, pens, and school supplies. I think there was even a slap bracelet in there.

At this point it did seem a little out of the ordinary, but they were being so *nice*. I thanked them and skipped off to recess, giggling at what a good day it was turning out to be.

An hour later, I walked back into the classroom. Maria and her accomplice were standing off to the side of the room, speaking in hushed tones with our substitute. After a few minutes, I was called over from my desk.

This time there were no fun birthday presents behind his back. His hands stood clasped in front of him, empty, as he told me that I had to return Maria and her friend's things that I had taken.

Taken?

"No, it was a *present*," I tried to explain.

The girls denied it.

The substitute didn't punish me. He chalked the whole thing up to a misunderstanding—I think he knew. But nevertheless, I had to walk back to my desk, empty the contents of my hat, and give all the school supplies back to the two girls whilst they giggled behind their hands.

I felt as hollow as my now-empty bowler hat, sitting on the bus heading home that afternoon.

But it wasn't because of the presents I had to return. I didn't need the pencils, or the highlighters, or even the slap bracelet.

It was the experience of feeling special, feeling appreciated, and then realizing it was all a façade.

When I finally moved out on my own, I was left with a lot of empty space. I spent my days alone with my own thoughts, and I started realizing just how many of them were negative. My past was running my life.

And underneath the obvious bad events, like my mom dying, or bouncing from house to house during COVID, there were more subtle negative memories that came to the surface, like the memory of my second-grade birthday. I share it to illustrate that even seemingly innocuous moments from our childhood can have a monumental impact on our kid brains, and start to shape how we perceive the world and our place in it. Small memories like this, over time, left an impression on my little child's brain that festered into deep feelings of unworthiness and inability to take up space, which have pervaded my brain to this day, even as a twenty-three-year-old adult.

This is what I call one of my core wounds. My feeling of unworthiness.

We all have core memories from our childhood. They dictate our personality. What we like, how we act—it can all be tied back to these core memories. *And your core memories make no distinction between good and bad.*

This is what happened to me. My unworthiness wound sat in the depths of my subconscious, calling all the actions behind the scenes without my knowing.

This started around the time I was ten or eleven, the time when other people's perceptions of you start to solidify. I think that was when I first began to stray from the happy, bubbly kid I once was, to an anxious one, desperate for attention. Because I was always the one on the edge of the playground. Ostracized and targeted for reasons I didn't understand. Voted out of friend groups.

Beginning to look at life through a dreary gray lens of exclusion, all my memories now served to reinforce that belief—the belief that I am not worth the space that my existence demands.

My distorted sense of self and inability to cultivate my own self-worth, meant that I began to subconsciously look for proof of my worth outside of myself.

We chase feelings.

This tendency manifested as chasing relationships and approval, limerence, intense people pleasing, and endlessly trying to conform for people to like me. *But trying to conform for approval only reaffirmed to myself that I was not worthy to show up in the world as I truly was.*

Chasing approval clouded my decision making and led me into unsafe situations, especially as a teen. I would lie to my parents, go out to drink, and hang out with boys older than me.

It was during this time that my intimacy was violated without consent for the first time. By someone I liked.

I know that no one causes their own sexual assault. I know that I always have the right to my own autonomy no matter where I am, what I am doing, or what I wear. But at the time my self-esteem was so low that I blamed myself. I hated myself for drinking. I hated myself for trusting him. I hated myself for my inability to speak up. I was so *ashamed.*

This shame became my constant companion. Every negative interaction I had became further evidence of my belief that I was undeserving. If someone didn't like me, I was upset, but it was a *familiar* upset. It reaffirmed the belief I had inside, because *I* didn't like me.

The real kicker was that even if someone *did* like me or give me a compliment, if someone gave me the approval I so desperately craved, I *still* didn't believe them. I couldn't receive any love or praise without feeling tense and uncomfortable, like bugs were crawling up my skin. It went against everything I had told myself.

This is where confirmation bias comes into play. Our brains like to look for evidence, but they tend to cherry-pick the evidence that goes along with our existing beliefs. And for as long as I can remember, I had been operating hopelessly glass half empty.

Every time I was faced with rejection, I thought, *No one wants me, what is wrong with me?* Every time I was faced with praise or acceptance, I thought, *I don't believe you.*

My brain was obsessed with this victim narrative I had identified with my entire life, fixating on the evidence that affirmed it, and completely disregarding anything that challenged its hypothesis.

If I wanted anything to change, if I wanted to find love, happiness, and fulfillment without being at the whims of other people, I needed to rewrite my story.

The first step to rewriting my story was accepting and forgiving "Trauma Heather."

Trauma Heather is the term I coined for the person I became out of my negative experiences. The me who made decisions out of survival mode. The me who lacked all boundaries and self-respect when seeking approval. The me who abandoned herself in the quest to prove that she deserved to exist.

I held so much *shame.* That was why I hadn't been able to face my past all these years. Because facing my past meant coming to terms with the fact that *I had become someone I didn't like when I looked in the mirror.*

I *had* to find a way to let go of the shame if I was ever going to move forward. What I really needed was understanding.

So I got off my bed and locked eyes with myself in the mirror.

"Heather, *it makes sense* that you quieted yourself and dulled your thoughts and your boundaries, because you were scared of the reactions of other people. *It makes sense* that you pursued shitty relationship after shitty relationship, because you just wanted to feel loved. *It makes sense* that you were controlling in friendships, because unpredictability did not feel safe to you. *It makes sense* that you turned to drugs and alcohol, because you just wanted a reprieve from the negative confines of your mind. *It makes sense …*"

I took a deep breath and then continued, sympathy and grief dancing together through my green eyes.

"It makes sense that you wanted to go out and be around the boy that you liked. It makes sense that you were drinking—that's what people in high school do. It wasn't your fault. *It wasn't your fault.*"

My voice broke. I closed my eyes for a few moments before I continued.

"And I love you, and I'm so sorry for everything you had to go through, and I know you were always just doing what you thought was best, but everything's okay because *I am here now and we are going to make things better.*"

I sat back on my bed. Only once I had acceptance and understanding for how I had operated in the past, only once I showed *every* part of myself love, could I move on to step two. Acquiring evidence.

My brain had learned to only look at the negative, so I had to learn to think differently. I had to start looking at the positive. I tried to remember, to write down things people had said, and interactions I'd had that pointed to the fact that I *am* worthy. I *am* deserving. I *am* a good person.

I began to say these affirmations in the mirror every morning.

I am worthy. I am deserving. I am a good person.

When I first started this practice, I could feel my brain pushing back. It didn't want to leave its old ways. I felt like a stranger in my own skin. I would pierce my gaze through the mirror as if I was trying to slay an enemy—in a way, I was. But the enemy was myself.

"I am worthy."

Who do you think you are to say that?

"I am deserving."

Why would anyone believe that about you?

"I am a good person."

You're just telling lies to yourself.

When my brain resisted, I tried to remind myself of all the evidence I'd collected to the contrary.

It wasn't enough to just say these things out loud though. I needed to go out into the world and create new proof for these new beliefs.

That's what I had started to do when I was going to the beach by myself. Every time I went and tried something new and held my head up high, "acting like a confident person," it was more evidence to add to the *You are awesome!* folder, rather than the *You suck!* folder in my memory bank.

It was like a game—I was collecting little gold stars for my personality.

Eventually I branched out from the beach and began tackling all sorts of new situations on my own. I went to a trampoline park, to the movies, and one day on a whim, I wiped my Instagram and started posting anything I felt like posting, using my authentic voice rather than curating myself for anyone else. Every time I posted my thoughts unfiltered, I was reaffirming to my mind: *I deserve to take up space exactly as I am.*

Whenever I walk into a space with my shoulders back, whenever I accept a compliment without being bashful and saying, "Oh me? Nooo," whenever I share my honest opinion, whenever I try something new, whenever I show kindness to someone and am met with warmth in return, I'm creating more and more proof for my brain that I am worthy, I deserve to take up space, and I am *safe* when I do it.

I still do my affirmations every day, but now I've started to say them with a smile on my face and warmth in my heart, because I'm finally beginning to *believe* what I'm saying as I look into the mirror.

I'm not going to lie and tell you that this core wound is suddenly gone and I never feel it now, because that's not true. Healing is difficult—it takes time and it is not always linear. But I *can* tell you that in doing all this, I have never seen such rapid growth in myself, in my confidence, in my courage, and in my willingness to enter spaces I never would have felt I deserved to be a part of in the past.

Like the published author circle!

Trauma Heather was being laid to rest. I could not have imagined the rapid mindset shifts that came when I fully committed to this. My soul was starting to come back online.

WHY

I almost didn't get an A in math, but then Mr.
Carlo told me to stop asking "why?" all the time
and just follow the formulas. So, I did. Now, I get
perfect scores on all my tests. I just wish I knew
what the formulas did. I honestly have no idea.
—Stephen Chbosky, *The Perks of
Being a Wallflower*

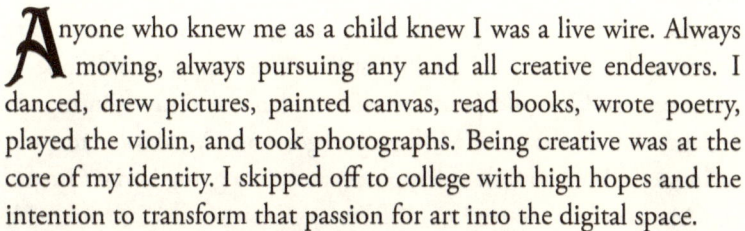

Anyone who knew me as a child knew I was a live wire. Always moving, always pursuing any and all creative endeavors. I danced, drew pictures, painted canvas, read books, wrote poetry, played the violin, and took photographs. Being creative was at the core of my identity. I skipped off to college with high hopes and the intention to transform that passion for art into the digital space.

My mom was my biggest supporter. She always encouraged me to pursue art, regardless of the pervasive starving artist stereotypes in our culture. She was so excited for this next chapter in my life. To celebrate the occasion, she wrote me a send-off letter. It was written inside a card decorated with one of my old drawings.

A neon-striped bird adorned with purple boots and a pink cowboy hat graced the cover. He stood on a red nest in a tree, a tree where all the branches were multicolored neon curly Qs.

I had no idea my mom still had a copy of it.

This letter is my most prized possession. In it, Mom expressed gratitude for our relationship, advice for my life to come, and the reassurance that she was always there should I need anything while on this new journey.

On the back of the letter, *Artist's Name* was written in type, with *Heather Rutishauser* scrawled out below in Sharpie and my third-grade lettering. Above, my mom's cursive continued. So many words to be said they could not be contained within the folds of the card:

P.S. As you start an exciting career in digital design, I thought this card with one of your earliest art designs would be most appropriate :)

That was the last sentence she ever wrote. She had her stroke on the car ride home after dropping me off at college that day.

Mom's death shifted everything I knew about the world. Thrust into an unfamiliar environment and overwhelmed by grief, my entire personality shifted.

Even throughout high school, as I struggled with deep insecurity issues under the surface, I could still be the happy, bubbly one in the room, and I would pour myself into dance and my painting. At college, all that was gone. My light had gone out. My days were spent trying to uphold a mask of happiness and then going home to cry.

My creativity started to drift away. Creative assignments with open-ended parameters began to fill me with dread. I needed explicit instructions I could follow to the letter.

Creativity means diving into the unknown. The unknown was no longer a safe place for me.

As time went on, my artistic identity shrank into a shell, and I migrated more and more behind the camera. I loved photography and video—I still do—but I think staying only in that medium was a crutch. I was just pointing at what I saw with my lens and hitting record, rather than assuming my position as a creator, opening up a conversation between my visions, my tools, and my environment.

I graduated college feeling completely lost and unsure of where to go next because I had become so disconnected from the core of who I am. I hadn't painted anything in the four years since my mom had passed, I hadn't drawn in three, I hadn't read for pleasure in God knows how long, and I certainly hadn't been writing.

I only had a vague conception of what to do with my life, but I needed a job, so I didn't take the time to reflect on what I wanted. I just jumped into an artist-adjacent field that I had a transferable skill set for: journalism.

I became a broadcast news photographer.

On paper it made sense. *She has great camera skills and she loves to tell stories!*

In reality, it was deadening my soul.

Because I had become a shadow artist. Yes, I was using my camera, but not in the way I wanted to. Not with the freedom and control that my creative spirit was calling for. My trauma had blocked my creativity so much that I woke up one day and found myself on a completely unaligned career path.

I think it was a necessary step for that time in my life. I was focused on surviving. I needed a job where I could just follow orders, and follow them well. But being a creative at heart, I came to realize that I had chosen this path to avoid working through my pain. Which is why once I was ready to face my pain, it all fell away.

I had left that job for only a week and a half when I got the urge to paint again. Nothing fancy, just a little sign for my apartment.

But I hadn't painted anything in *five years*. I can't tell you how freeing it was just to make the first brush stroke. It was as liberating as the moment I spoke my mom's name out loud in my apartment just a few weeks earlier. Another chain broken in my mind.

I moved my hand back and forth, becoming reacquainted with the rhythm and flow of the brush, blending colors, and creating shapes. I flipped open the cap of a green paint bottle and slowly squeezed some more pigment onto a paper towel. After a moment, drops of liquid falling down began to mix with the pigment.

I was crying.

My creativity is at the very core of who I am. And I had suppressed it for so *long*. It felt like I had been asleep for the past five years since my mom had passed.

A ghost, a zombie, the walking dead.

And those five years had directly coincided with my first five years of adulthood. So in some ways, it felt as if I was just now turning eighteen.

The more I create, the more I can feel my soul coming to life, the more I remember who I was as a child, and the more I feel in touch with who I am meant to be as an adult.

And in that moment, it really did feel as if I was meeting my adult self for the first time. Because the person I had been for the past five years was not me. It was someone else—Trauma Heather—desperate to survive.

This was Heather. I was excited to get to know her.

This was the curious phenomenon that occurred as I began to reintegrate parts of myself I had lost to trauma, and recover from the stress of my professional job; I started to tap back into my creativity and childlike joy.

I looked around at the world with wonder. I stopped to smell flowers and I marveled at every spider's web. I played hopscotch every time I passed the chalk outline by my house. I blasted music and danced around my apartment. My previously dark mind became filled with inspiration and new ideas.

At the root of creativity is curiosity, and that's all we ever are as children: curious. We experiment and we play, trying to understand why things are the way they are. We question *everything*—sometimes much to our parents' annoyance.

Why? Why? Why?

But as adults, we're already programmed. *This is the way the world works.*

We're not supposed to question it. That's against the unspoken rules.

So we stop asking questions. We start operating on autopilot. We stay in our comfort zones because we're worried of being perceived as outside the norm.

I missed the unwritten memo that I wasn't supposed to do that when I got older. I've always had an insatiable mind that I have never been able to switch off. I question everything to this day. I always need to know the *Why*.

In high school, this became "challenging authority." At home as well. One of my teachers used to say that I would make a great lawyer, because I was always debating.

It wasn't my intention. I would simply see systems that were working in a way that didn't make sense to me, justified because that was just "the way things were."

I hate that argument.

In the workforce, my queries turned from being interpreted as "challenging authority," to "immaturity" and "lack of intelligence." Because apparently, I asked *too* many questions. Coworkers and supervisors at various jobs would chuckle at my naive enthusiasm and joke about limiting the number of questions I could ask in a given period of time. It made me feel inferior and ashamed.

I began to feel increasingly bad about myself, because it was clear to me from others' reactions that this wasn't the norm. But I just kept wondering how are others *not* asking this many questions? How are others *not* questioning every single possible outcome for a given scenario and making sure they have the capabilities to handle each one? How are people *not* questioning every institution or rule we have created, why it was created that way, and what we can do to make it better?

I think true naivety is sitting in what you *think* you know and never questioning it. No change was ever brought forth by quietly accepting the status quo.

For this reason, I believe children are the wisest among us. They refuse to take things at society's face value, and instead see what is *actually there.*

This is the most valuable skill you could ever have. And yet, we drill it out of our kids as they get older, through the rigid conformity of the bell system and multiple-choice testing that teaches us that there is always only *one* right answer to every problem.

If we could simply learn to look at our world through the eyes of a child, we would rapidly evolve as a society.

After I finished painting, I set down my brush and took a walk down the beach. I sat for a while on a rock overlooking the ocean, observing people the way I used to back when I pretended that I was a spy with my little composition notebook.

A mom stood on a nearby stretch of beach, dutifully keeping an eye on her toddler as they scrambled about on a rock. I glanced at the child and saw their wide-open eyes—a marker of innocence, of an intense curiosity about the unfamiliar world.

Oh how I wish I could become like that child again, I thought to myself. *A live wire of curiosity, before society descended to tell me what I ought to be.*

I am trying to unlearn this programming. I am trying to become okay with being myself, even when that means that I am messy and unpredictable. Even when that means that I am questioning the realities that others take for granted.

"That's the way it is."

That's what you always hear when trying to make meaningful change.

"But it doesn't have to be that way!" I want to scream back.

It *doesn't* have to be that way.

PARADOXICAL

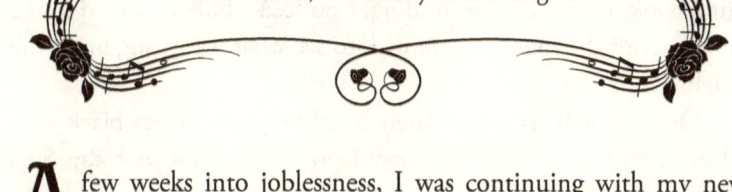

I suddenly see all the arguments and
the rest of it in a different light, and am
not as prejudiced as I was.
How can I have changed so much?
—Anne Frank, *The Diary of a Young Girl*

Afew weeks into joblessness, I was continuing with my new morning routine of journaling on the ocean rocks near my apartment. It was my one constant at a time where all other aspects of my life were shrouded in the unknown.

There was one morning that began like any other. I was stream of consciousness journaling for a half an hour or so. These entries were usually all over the place—a chaotic mix of anxious thoughts of unemployment and half-baked plans for how to spend the day, with some occasional deep philosophical reflections about life sprinkled in. I unearthed one of those deeper musings in my brain on that very morning. Here is what I wrote:

> *I think I've taken a lot of things for granted in the past. I don't want to do that anymore. Yes, I need to acknowledge my struggles and shouldn't discount them, but it's that yin and yang. My life has not only been full of struggle but of immense privilege. It took me a while to realize that one of the hallmarks of true maturity is realizing that there*

can be two coinciding truths at the same time. I can have really struggled, but still be very fortunate. Someone could be right in their argument, but wrong in the way they approach communicating about it. Yin and yang.

I finished my last few words, slipped my journal back into my bag, and began to walk back to my apartment. On my way home, I saw a café and decided to stop in. I was still new to this area of San Diego, and I had never been there.

I ordered a sandwich, walked over to a corner table, and pulled out a book. Before I began reading, I noticed a bulletin board in the far corner of the room. I went over to see what was going on in the neighborhood.

One of the fliers immediately caught my eye. It was black with white lettering, and said *Take an Angel with you on your day.* Surrounding the edges of the flier were numerous rip-off tabs. Each one depicted a small abstract angel line drawing, and below it, a name.

I wouldn't have given a second glance to this type of flier in the past. But now I knew that angels were real, so I decided to pick one, and carry their blessing with me.

I took a minute to scan the various names. They were not the standard Christian angel names. I had not heard of any of them before. So I just picked the one that was calling out to me.

Janusia.

I stuck her in my sweater, went back to my table, and began reading.

About an hour later, I was making my way home from the café when I stuck my hand into my pocket and felt a sliver of paper.

Janusia.

I had completely forgotten about her.

I held out the small image in one hand and my phone in the other. I wanted to know who this Janusia was.

I searched "janusia angel." Not much came up. I couldn't find any specific article about an angel with that name, like I was expecting.

What did pop up on my search results was an article about something called Janusian thinking.

What was Janusian thinking? I wondered. I had never heard of it before.

I clicked on the article to read more. As I read, my steps started getting slower and slower, until soon I had completely stopped in the middle of the sidewalk.

Because apparently, like the concept of yin and yang, Janusian thinking is the practice of being able to visualize two opposite concepts existing at the same time. It was named after the Roman god Janus, who represents duality. Images of Janus show a man with two faces, looking in opposite directions.

I stared at the angel. Then back at my phone. Then back at the angel again.

Two contradictory ideas existing at the same time?

Had I not just randomly written about that concept not even two hours ago?

I ran back to my apartment and pulled out my journal. I already knew the words were sitting there waiting for me because I had *just* written them, but I still needed to confirm it. Because it felt like I was losing my mind. I reread the page, and then slowly leaned back in my chair.

The synchronicities were happening in my thoughts now.

What is going on?

I dropped the journal and put my head in my hands.

Am I going crazy?

Past the surface level of this story concerning the bizarre psychic happenings in my brain, I want to dive deeper into the concept of Janusian thinking, because it is an important one. Clearly the universe thought so as well, affirming it to me through this angel.

Our society is steeped in conflict—divided and reactive. This is because the majority of us do not have the capacity or awareness to engage in Janusian thinking. We have a tendency to be rigid, so stuck in our ways that we aren't able to see the possibility of two perspectives coexisting.

This used to be me. My self-concept was so low that I couldn't handle anyone challenging my perception of reality. Everything had to be black and white, like the angel poster tacked to the wall that day.

This is what creates conflicts in relationships. Looking back, a countless number of times the conflicts I have had with others have been based on miscommunication and differing expectations, rather than one person being wrong and the other right.

We all have our own ways of perceiving reality. The goal should never be to decide which person's reality is the one truth. That is an impossible task. The goal, rather, should be to rectify the ways in which the reality we've created in our own mind *might be based on assumptions of the other.* We must fully see our reality—as well as theirs—in order to reach a mutual understanding. People who always strive to be right in an argument, value their ego more than their relationships.

For example, you're upset that your roommate has not cleaned the apartment. You automatically assume that this says something about their character. That they're lazy, or they don't respect you, and you get upset. This generates emotions that *blind* you to the person standing in front of you.

Because here's the thing, you have a *right* to want the apartment clean, but you actually have *no idea* why it isn't. Maybe your roommate had a really rough day at work, maybe they're struggling with executive dysfunction, maybe they have so much on their plate that they simply forgot, or maybe they have a huge deadline tomorrow and are planning to clean right after they meet it.

But what if *both* you and your roommate's realities are true? What if you have a right to have the apartment clean, *and* your roommate is struggling at work? Acknowledging both truths and releasing the need for just one person to be right, is how you release the negative emotions and judgment that have built up pressure around the situation. It's how you find not just compromise, but *collaboration*.

Our inability to acknowledge coexisting opposites is also what prevents us from creating meaningful change within ourselves.

We all tell ourselves stories about who we are, what we stand for, and what we believe in. We reject anything that doesn't fit this narrative. But we as humans are *walking contradictions*. We are meant to change, grow, learn, and adapt. Rather than trying to keep up with this perfect façade of who we believe we are, we need to wholeheartedly embrace the fact that we are multi-faceted beings. That we can make mistakes and also learn from them. That we can say things one day, and then completely change our minds. That we can completely reinvent ourselves.

That we can *rewrite our stories*.

We refuse to see both sides of the coin. We refuse to let go of the past versions of ourselves to be reborn anew. *But we have to let parts of ourselves die in order to live.* We have to come face to face with our own contradictions and decide who we want to be. We have to decide what boxes we want to begin to open, and what lines we want to completely obliterate.

I cannot tell you the absolute freedom I have felt from embracing the fact that my existence is a paradox. I am not, and will never be, easily digestible for the masses.

I have been a liar and a truth teller. I have been a follower and a leader. I have been a consumer and a creator. I have been the girl too petrified to speak, and I have been the girl lifting up a room of hundreds with her voice. I have played it safe, and I have fearlessly run full speed off the cliff. A reader and an author. A taker and a giver. A fight starter and a peacemaker. A victim and a warrior. I have been full of hate, and I am now full of love.

Such is the duality of life. What are you?

THE ISLAND OF
MISFIT TOYS

And in that moment, I swear we were infinite.
—Stephen Chbosky, *The Perks of
Being a Wallflower*

Sometimes I look back on my childhood and get concerned that it's mostly one big blank. There's glimpses … my fourth grade Camp Rock backpack … playing four-square on the black top during recess.

I have a lot of these flash-type memories, sometimes triggered by sensations in the current moment. But in terms of actual events—full, drawn-out scenes—there is very little I consciously remember.

Almost all of what I do remember is painful. I feel the ringing in my ears, the laughter of others at my expense. For as long as I can remember, I could never understand why I was the butt of every joke. I had always been a dysfunctional magnet, drawing people in to become the object of their negativity and pain.

The most vivid of these school memories took place in Mrs. Barry's classroom. Fifth grade.

I walked through the doorway to find a handful of my classmates gathered around the student mailboxes, snickering. A boy named Sharuf was having his birthday soon. Piled in his hand was a stack of freshly printed invitations.

A birthday party!

One of the main events we look forward to as eleven-year-olds—a reprieve from the mundanity of the classroom.

Sharuf pulled out invite after invite, sliding them into the wooden mail slots adorned with each student's name. This was the fifth grade—one of the last years your parents still have you invite everyone in the class to your birthday party.

When Sharuf finished, he turned around, and proudly proclaimed to the group of onlookers that he had invited everyone in the class …

His eyes shifted toward mine, a wicked grin on his face.

… but me.

I turned to the cardstock sticking out of the rows of boxes. My gaze landed on the slot that said *Heather*.

Empty.

I wished he had done the big reveal at the end of the day. At least then I could've gone straight home on the bus. Instead, I sat there for the next eight hours, eyes glued to the nametag on my desk, feeling the gaze of everyone in the class burn into the back of my head.

I willed myself to disappear.

It didn't work.

Sometimes I find myself wondering, if the few stories like this are the only things I remember from my childhood, then what are the countless other memories my mind has willed me to forget?

This memory lapse has happened in other facets of my life too. It is an incredibly dissonant feeling every time my sisters say, "Remember when …"—only to recall something I have no recollection of.

How odd and paradoxical was my identity crisis, to feel so tied down by my past, and yet only have vague visions of the lives I've lived before this moment.

The memories may not have all been there, but the conditioning remained. I remember telling my therapist—multiple times *and* multiple therapists—that I didn't like to be perceived. I would flap my hands, shake my head, and grimace as if I had just sipped some sour milk.

Just the *thought* of being perceived was too much.

Why was I so afraid of being seen? I'm realizing now, it's because the only times I received people's full attention, were moments like these. All other times, I flew under the radar, did what I was told ... *sweet little girl, teacher's pet.* But God forbid I made a mistake, I was yelled at by my parents. When I was myself at school, I was singled out, isolated, and bullied.

The more I grew up, the more I withered away. I became a pawn on a chess board—unable to move, paralyzed in fear.

Better to stay on the sidelines. I was used to it. I was the girl who doesn't get invited to birthday parties.

The Girl Who Doesn't Get Invited to Birthday Parties.

This was another story I had been unknowingly living in. Even as an adult, I never wanted to do anything to stand out, like I did standing in Mrs. Barry's classroom that day.

But that was changing.

Slowly but surely, *The Girl Who Doesn't Get Invited to Birthday Parties,* was turning into *The Girl Who Throws Her Own Parties, Whether You Decide to Join or Not.*

The more I took risks, the more I forced myself to do things alone while in the presence of other people, the more comfortable I became with being perceived by others. I now walked with straight posture and no longer automatically felt inferior to those around me. I was caring less and less about what people thought. The limits in my mind were slowly, but surely, melting away.

One of these days I was walking down the sidewalk along the shoreline by my apartment, when I came across a teenage boy, standing on a concrete block and playing electric violin. Below him were three women, all middle aged, dancing and floating around on the sidewalk. With eyes closed, they were spinning and twirling and moving, it seemed, without a single care in the world.

It wasn't a performance. They weren't in costume. They had simply stopped to dance to the music.

Surrounding this magical scene was a larger group of people. They were standing still, watching, many filming the scene on their phones.

While this spontaneous display of human expression may have been a normal thing to see over at Ocean Beach—which is a much more free-spirited part of San Diego—there were a lot of tourists around that day. I could sense the crowd, see the scan of their eyes over the women. I deeply felt the aura of judgment, of spectacle, rather than of awe and support.

Of course there was judgment. These women, just randomly twirling and dancing on the sidewalk?

How *weird*.

At least that's what I would've thought to myself a few months ago.

Instead, I found myself leaning against a palm tree, my eyes fluttering back and forth as I watched these women, entranced, desperately wanting to join them.

I was *done* conditioning myself to be a background character. I looked around at the crowd of people surrounding me. They were *standing still*.

These women were floating in the air.

I no longer wanted to be a watcher. I wanted to *live*. I wanted to *fly*.

So when one of the women beckoned me to join the circle, I thought, *Fuck it*. I set my backpack on the ground, kicked off my sandals, and entered the large empty space—knowing that the crowd was now watching *my* every move.

I began to sway and spin, and immediately felt so blissful. I have always loved dancing. I took dance classes my entire life.

But then college became After.

I stopped dancing. My movements became hardened. My emotions became stuck in my body. I moved slowly and mechanically and struggled with daily chronic pain.

In this moment, however, I tapped back into the me I was in my childhood ballet class. I moved with strength but also with flow. I forgot about everyone around me and only listened to my body, just doing what felt good. The more I moved, the more joy I felt. My bare toes grazed the asphalt as my arms made shapes through the air.

After a song or two, I once again became aware of the eyes surrounding me. But instead of fear or anxiety setting in, I started not to care.

In a way, I even began to feel sad. I wondered if there was anyone else out there in that crowd who desperately wanted to dance but was too afraid to let themselves be seen.

Maybe my dancing could inspire them to dance too.

There are so many people in this world, unable to do the things they truly want to do, because the fear of judgment keeps them in a cage. Some of them even judge others for stepping out of the norm, because they are too afraid to do it themselves.

That was who I used to be.

But no longer.

I continued to dance. I stayed there for over two hours, on that main street with dozens of people passing by, as the sun set and night overtook the sky. I didn't want to leave. I couldn't get enough of this feeling. This feeling of doing whatever *I* wanted to do in front of others and *not caring*.

It is one of life's greatest highs.

The longer I stayed, the more people joined us. By the end of the night, we had a whole ragtag group, all dancing and having the time of our lives on that sidewalk. It had me thinking about all the people I may have missed out on connecting with in the past because my social conditioning had taught me to write off those who went against the grain.

I got home that night, hours later than intended. I shut the door to my apartment and leaned my back against it, a smile slowly creeping across my face.

I felt so *free*.

In that moment, I realized it was a feeling completely foreign to me. I had spent my whole life dictating my actions around how I *thought* I would be perceived by *other people*. I had placed myself in my *own* mental prison.

I felt a twinge of mourning as I thought back on all the times in my past where I had stood still, watching *others* live. A bystander, scared into submission.

So much of my energy, *wasted*. So much of my life, *wasted*. So many moments, putting stock into what *other people* were going to think, instead of caring about what *I* think about *myself*.

I was done letting my life be dictated by other people. It was time to start living.

I finally peeled myself away from the door as tears formed in my eyes.

I feel like young Heather is looking up at me and smiling so big right now. All she ever wanted to do was dance.

I'm Ready

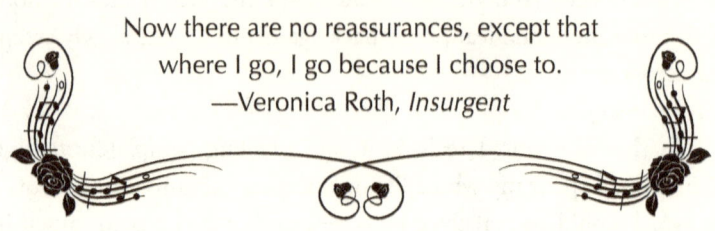

Now there are no reassurances, except that
where I go, I go because I choose to.
—Veronica Roth, *Insurgent*

When I was dancing with this ragtag group of misfits, an older man approached and started spinning his way toward me. He had tattered pants cut off just below the knees and a graphic tee littered with holes near the bottom.

We danced for a bit, and he spun me around a few times. He seemed like a kind soul; I'd been learning to not judge a book by its cover.

After a few minutes, he commented that I had a unique aura around me. Then he asked me about the brown beaded bracelet I was wearing on my right arm.

I hadn't had it for long. I was drawn to it at a garage sale a few weeks back, and instinctively began wearing it every day.

Everything connects back to those garage sales!

He told me that he used to regularly attend the Buddhist temple down the street, and what I was wearing was a Buddha bracelet. I told him how funny that was because I hadn't known the meaning of the bracelet when I had gotten it, but lately I was becoming more open to the idea of spirituality and meditation.

After a few more minutes of spinning around to the violin melody, the man spoke up again. He said something to me that felt cryptic, but at the same time, profound. It felt as if Spirit itself was moving through this man as he uttered his next words.

"When the student is ready, the master appears."

He didn't elaborate.

Later that night, I said my goodbyes to the other dancers and walked back to my apartment. Before I went to bed, I scrolled on Tik Tok for a few minutes. A random tarot reading popped up on my feed, but when my eyes skimmed the caption, I stopped and stared.

When the student is ready, the teacher appears.

Slightly different wording, but *same exact message*. I now know that this sentiment comes from the *Tao Te Ching*, but at the time, I had never heard it before.

Now here it was, appearing *twice*, in only the span of a few hours?

I knew enough by now to know that there are no coincidences.

I woke up the next day with that cryptic message drifting through the back of my mind. And then I was inevitably on Tik Tok again.

This really *is* a spiritual awakening story in the twenty-first century.

A young man that I had never seen before, popped up on my For You Page. He had short, curly brown hair and a crystal dangling from his neck. He was sitting on an ATV in what looked like the middle of a jungle.

His name was Kai.

In the video, he described how he had dropped out of college to start a business, and how, now, he was financially free and living his dream life, helping others do the same. He said to message him if I was interested in building a personal brand.

So I messaged him.

What do I have to lose?

I looked up at the vision board I had created, now hanging on my wall. I felt I had important knowledge to share. I felt like I had the potential to help people. I had gone through struggles and I felt a deep calling to help guide others through the same. And I had been posting on social media for a bit, but I was struggling to gain any traction. Maybe this guy could help.

We messaged back and forth, which eventually led to me scheduling a call with him for a few days later.

I wasn't naive. I knew that if I got on that call, this dude was going to try to sell me something. So the night before our meeting, I decided to go back to his Instagram page, to decide if this was *really* someone I wanted to work with.

I navigated to his account and read his bio.

I help professionals reprogram their subconscious.

Interesting …

I scrolled down a bit further and clicked on the very first pinned post on his profile. As I read the caption, I realized that it was a client testimonial.

"Before working with Kai I was stressed and wasn't progressing, now I feel good with the routine and am motivated to progress each day."

The caption continued, but my heart stopped as I read the next line.

When Laura came to me …

Laura.

My *mom's name.*

Laura isn't the most common name. In the five years since my mom had passed, it almost never crossed my path.

But ever since I had said her name out loud that one night, sitting alone in my apartment, I started to see her name *everywhere*. I began to follow where her name led me, as another one of my signs.

Well now, it had led me right to Kai.

And I *still* couldn't shake the phrase stuck in my head, spoken by the mysterious man at the dance circle the previous night.

When the student is ready, the master appears.

Call me crazy, but I took all this as a sign that if the meeting with

Kai went well, if I trusted him, if I thought he could help get me to where I wanted to be, and my only concern was financial, then it was time for me to take some leaps and invest in myself.

Well, the next day the call did go well. And I did trust him. So I signed on to work together.

No more safety net. No more turning back.

It was time to see where putting faith in myself and my voice would lead me.

Learning to Fish

At first people refuse to believe that a strange
new thing can be done, then they begin to
hope it can be done, then they see it can
be done—then it is done and all the world
wonders why it was not done centuries ago.
—Frances Hodgson Burnett,
The Secret Garden

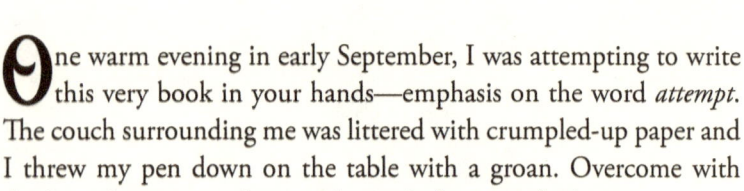

One warm evening in early September, I was attempting to write this very book in your hands—emphasis on the word *attempt*. The couch surrounding me was littered with crumpled-up paper and I threw my pen down on the table with a groan. Overcome with doubt and resistance, I stepped outside for some fresh air.

I was feeling called to the ocean lately. There is peace and serenity in witnessing a force larger than yourself. I found myself magnetically drawn to the end of the pier, like I was following a siren's call.

I walked along the waves and a man stepped right in front of me. He said, "I'm going to teach you how to fish."

Although this was strange, I could tell his intentions were pure. And I was actively trying to welcome new life experiences. So I agreed, even though the offer was *very* random.

He handed me a pole, showed me how to cast it, and soon enough the lure was floating off somewhere in the distance. He walked back over to his friend who was fishing on the other side of the pier.

I stood there, fishing for the first time in my life.

Staring out at the expanse of blue, I began to reflect on how far I'd come. In the past, I never would've been able to do something like this. To just sit with the energy of the ocean, and dive deep into my own mind. Fishing never seemed enjoyable to me. It seemed boring.

What do you do while you wait?

The truth is, I used to be scared to sit alone with my thoughts. Empty space was room for my demons to dance in. But lately I was undergoing a shift. The demons drifted away and empty space became room for artful words, rhythmic sentences, and deep reflections about the meaning of life.

I smiled, as I realized I was finally starting to feel at home in my own mind, instead of trying to escape it. I began to crave the endless possibilities that sit in the vastness of empty space.

And I was grateful for the fishing. It allowed me time to reflect, to be writing these realizations now.

After about twenty minutes, the fisherman—his name was Chino—approached me again. He took out his phone and started tapping on the screen.

"I'm going to play some music for you, so you don't have to sit in silence."

"That's okay. I like sitting in my own thoughts," I replied automatically.

His next remark stopped me in my tracks.

"That means you're an artist. You need to write that stuff down."

I smiled.

I'm sure you've heard the saying "go with the flow." I had recently discovered that this phrase is not just a fun colloquialism, but in fact one of the most important principles for living a fulfilling life.

Staring out at the ocean, I realized that we can learn a lot from water. Life comes in waves. We have to learn to *ride* them.

Most of our suffering comes from trying to swim upstream,

trying to fight the current. Our human tendency to build up expectations around people, events, and our entire life, leads to discontent. When our expectations aren't met, we get upset, we react. This makes us miss out on some of the most beautiful experiences in life. We have to release expectations and respond to what is in front of us. We have to live in flow.

In the past few weeks, I kept thinking back to a line I had read about effortless action—a Taoist principle. Taoism is a Chinese philosophy, and *The Te of Piglet* by Benjamin Hoff describes the principles of Taoism through Winnie the Pooh characters:

> "Effortless Action. That's something the Taoists say we can learn by watching water."
> "Water?" asked Piglet.
> "When a stream comes to some stones in its path, it doesn't struggle to remove them, or fight against them, or *think* about them. It just goes around them. And as it does, it sings. Water responds to What's There with effortless action."

Responding to *What's There*. This seemed like an easy enough principle to follow. But in reality, I realized that my mind loved to cloud *What's There* with illusions and expectations.

This night on the pier was a prime example. In the past, if a man approached me, telling me he was going to teach me how to fish, I probably would have said no and kept walking. I had an expectation in my mind of how my pier walk would go and when I would get home, and this man's unexpected offer would've interfered with that. Or I would have thought that he was weird and brushed him off. Or maybe I would have said yes, cast the pole one time, and then kept going—thinking to myself, *I have places to be and things to do*.

If any of these scenarios had happened, I would have missed out on one of the most meaningful conversations I'd had in a long time. I would have missed out on some of the most profound life lessons I had learned on my journey thus far.

And you, fair reader, would have missed out on these next two chapters of my book.

I continued to talk to Chino. I liked picking his brain. He was a very deep, philosophical thinker, like myself.

We stood with our poles hanging over the ocean as he talked to me about fishing.

"Fishing is a way of life," he started. "We don't always get what we want, but we have to be patient with what we get blessed with. If we do this, eventually we will be thrust into abundance."

Patience …

I hadn't had too much of that in the past.

As he spoke, I couldn't help but reflect on my own life, which exhibited anything but patience. Our society today is a society of instant gratification. Fast food, get-rich-quick schemes, fifteen-second videos on Tik Tok. It lowers our patience and our drive—it lowered mine. Not only that, but my negative past experiences had me grasping at dopamine wherever I could get it, which led to a myriad of unhealthy coping mechanisms.

I still remember the reality check I had when reading the Tigger chapter in *The Te of Piglet*. The chapter of Tiggers is the chapter of instant gratification seekers. Hoff writes:

The major lesson that Tiggers need to learn is that if they don't control their impulses, their impulses will control them. No matter how much they do, Tiggers are never satisfied because they don't know the feeling of accomplishment that eventually comes when one persistently applies one's will to the attaining of not-immediately-reachable goals.

Wow …

That one stung—and gave a whole new meaning to the term

"paper cut."

I put down the book and sat for a few minutes, searching the recesses of my brain, trying to think of a time where I *really* committed to a not-immediately-reachable goal.

None came to mind.

I had a history of doing things that came naturally to me and avoiding the rest. I procrastinated on things when they stopped giving me the dopamine I craved. I abandoned projects when they showed me the least bit of resistance.

How much of my talent and skills were being wasted because I couldn't apply myself?

I had dreams, but I lacked discipline and commitment. Reading that quote, speaking to Chino, it was a wakeup call. If I was really going to start something new, to reach people, to make an impact, I had to learn patience and diligence.

I had to learn how to fish.

In quitting my job, pursuing my own business, posting on social media, and writing a book, I was, for the first time, committing myself to long-term goals. I sat in the discomfort of knowing that there would be no immediate payoff. Not only that, but knowing that there was absolutely no proof that there would ever even *be* a payoff.

I chose to sit and wait, move forward in a rowboat of faith, and believe in myself enough to know that I would eventually reach abundance.

This was a *very* scary place to sit.

But I could no longer live life as an unsatiated Tigger.

UNWISE

This lasted longer than I can describe even
if I wrote pages and pages about it.
—C.S. Lewis, *The Lion, the Witch
and the Wardrobe*

All light was now gone from the sky, and I was still stationed on the pier with a line dangling in the ocean. Chino was to my left, ten or fifteen feet away, and his friend was fishing across from us. A young couple came along, and Chino's friend offered to let them try to fish as well—I guess they did these spontaneous offers often. The couple agreed.

The friend said that he had a line that was guaranteed to catch them a fish. It was different from mine. I had a normal line with one hook on the end. This was one of those fishing lines that had about six hooks on it, all hanging from various heights. The only catch: the line was tangled.

The couple got to work untangling the fishing line.

I had been fishing for an hour or more at this point, sitting content in my own thoughts, when Chino approached me again. He pointed over toward the couple and said, "Those two are meant for each other."

I turned over my shoulder to look at the young man and woman across the pier.

"How do you know?" I questioned.

"They've been working on untangling that line for a half an hour," he explained. "Almost anyone else would have gotten frustrated and given up. They have patience. Whenever they come across something in life, whenever something crumbles, they will work together to untangle the mess."

I was amazed at Chino's observation. He wasn't just looking, but *seeing*. I peeled my eyes away from the couple and turned to Chino in awe.

"You're very wise," I said to him.

"No I'm not," he immediately fired back.

I paused. I wasn't expecting that response.

"Why do you say that?"

"The second you think you are wise," he explained, "Is the moment you don't know anything at all."

He was right. Admitting one is wise is falling prey to your ego. The smartest people in this world are the ones who can admit that they still have a lot to learn. The ones who are always searching, yearning for knowledge, and are not afraid to be contradicted or corrected. The ones who fully commit to being a lifelong student while here on this earth. To admit one is wise is to close yourself off to learning, to change. And to do that, is pure ignorance.

Chino's unwillingness to admit that he is wise, made him all the wiser in my eyes. I turned back to my line.

I began to get tired and pulled out my phone to look at the time—I had been fishing on the pier with Chino for almost three hours.

I laughed to myself. I had initially stopped and accepted Chino's spontaneous invitation to see if maybe, just maybe, I could catch a fish. But what I ended up getting from the experience was much more than that.

I reached a point, gazing out over the black expanse of ocean, where I didn't even *need* a fish anymore. I felt overwhelmingly full just from this raw human experience and conversation …

I felt a tugging on my pole and began reeling in the line. After a moment of resistance, the line raised to reveal a small little fishy, maybe three or four inches big, hanging off my hook.

I caught my very first fish!

How interesting are the laws of the universe, that the second I no longer *needed* the fish, was the second it appeared.

I have since learned that this principle applies to all areas of life.

I joyously held up my little fishy as Chino snapped a picture for me, and then I couldn't stop myself from jumping up and down with excitement.

My first fish!

As I jumped on that pier, staring at my fish and reflecting on my joy in that moment, I realized yet another life lesson. If I had gotten this fish on the first try, my first cast of the reel three hours ago, it wouldn't have felt so good. Hard work, determination, and patience were key ingredients in the recipe.

I know that the universe divinely guided me to fish with Chino that day. I had to experience, even in the smallest of capacities, the feeling of long-term gratification.

And it worked. I was done buying my fish from the market. I was going to fish for myself. Build my own life from the ground up.

However long it takes.

PRICELESS

> There is so much about my fate that I cannot
> control, but other things do fall under my
> jurisdiction ... I can decide how I spend my
> time, whom I interact with, whom I share my
> body and life and money and energy with. I
> can select what I eat and read and study ...
> And most of all, I can choose my thoughts.
> —Elizabeth Gilbert, *Eat Pray Love*

I learned how to manifest parking spots. It was working like a charm. When I first moved into my apartment, I was having to park three, sometimes four or five blocks away. Now, there was always at least one spot on my street, open without fail.

The key was that while driving home, I just visualized myself pulling right up to my apartment. I would keep saying to myself over and over in my head, *My parking spot is waiting there for me. I know it is.*

Well one day, it didn't work. I pulled up to a street lined with cars. I was a bit disappointed, but then I remembered everything I had learned about the way the universe operates.

Rejection is redirection.

If I wasn't parking in front of my apartment, it was for a reason.

I drove one street over and found a spot. I parked, got out of my car, and started walking down the block. I was not even one house down before I passed an elderly man peacefully sitting on his porch. He called out to me.

"What?" I hadn't understood what he said.

"Don't mind me, I'm just sitting here smoking weed on my porch," he repeated.

I laughed. "All power to you man. I don't judge," I remarked.

"You know this house is from the year 1919? It has the original interior and everything."

"Wow, does it really?"

I didn't know if I was that interested in historical houses, but I was just going along with the conversation.

"Yeah, do you want to see inside?" he offered.

Okay guys, I know how this sounds. Any other girl and elderly man, and this book could have a very different, much more abrupt ending. But I went into this man's house, and felt safe doing it, for two reasons.

One, at this point, I was becoming very attuned to people's energy fields. This was a sweet old man. I could sense his intentions. I could sense that there was no ill will, just genuine passion for his little historical home.

Two, I had just thought, *If I'm not parking in front of my apartment, then it's for a reason.* Now a man was inviting me to tour his house? That's not a normal everyday offer. So it must be heaven sent.

If I had learned anything from Chino the fisherman, it was that *it can be worthwhile to say yes to life sometimes.*

I walked up the porch steps and past the man, who was wearing a blue collared shirt and khaki shorts. His hair was stark white. I estimated he was somewhere in his eighties.

I stepped into the home, and before me was a small lounge area. Off this room, to the left was a bedroom, and to the right was the kitchen and a tiny back room with a washer and dryer. The entire place was the size of one large living room. For the next ten minutes or so, he walked me around the small space, talking about the architecture, the fact that it had an original HVAC system, etc.

Let's be honest here. Did I care much about the original HVAC system? No.

But he did.

I could feel the joy emanating from him, speaking about something he really loved. So I decided I would hold that space for him.

Eventually the conversation switched from architecture to his past experiences. He picked up a vintage photo of a man in front of an old airplane and began telling me about his adventures monitoring the color of the rice fields up in Sacramento.

As he spoke, I turned and looked over to the corner of the room. There was a beautiful mosaic lamp covered with roses. Hanging off its top was a necklace with an elephant pendant.

I complimented the necklace—elephants are my favorite animal.

He launched into a story about how the necklace was gifted to him from a member of a tribe in Africa, from when he had visited there. It was one of the most meaningful times in his life.

He looked at the necklace for a few moments, and then said, "Things like that are priceless."

A brief pause.

"The common man's priceless."

He went on to elaborate that the things he valued most in his life were not the things that cost him a lot of money, but the things that reminded him of the people and experiences that meant the most to him in his life.

As I heard him say all this, I felt chills travel down my spine. I knew this was yet another divine encounter.

I had begun to feel less and less attached to my material items. My giant pile of clothes, my growing Squishmallow collection, and all the online purchases that used to bring me joy, had instead begun to make me feel empty and weighed down. And here this man was, affirming the dissonance I was beginning to feel inside.

The common man's priceless.

The real things of value in life are not the things that we assign an exorbitant amount of material wealth to. They are not the things that hold meaning in the world of capitalism. That is all *made up*. The real things of value in this life are the things that hold deep meaning to us individually. The things that spark our memories, our humanity.

I left the porch of this man's house that day and walked around the corner to my apartment, deep in thought.

What are the things that I consider priceless?

Immediately I thought of Mom's letter. The one she wrote to me on the last day she was ever conscious. No amount of money could ever replace what that letter means to me.

But other than that letter, there wasn't much that came to mind.

I got home and stood in the center of the room, staring at everything in my apartment. It was *filled* with stuff. Clothes, shoes, knickknacks, bags, stuffed animals ... I'd always been a maximalist.

All of it was useless. *None* of it brought me fulfillment anymore. *None* of it meant anything to me anymore. I realized in that moment that I didn't want to continue collecting stuff that would weigh me down. I only wanted to keep what I truly valued. I wanted to feel lighter.

I grabbed random stuff and started piling it in the center of the room.

It was time to purge.

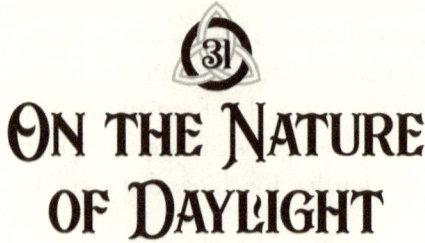

On the Nature of Daylight

Sit back and allow the words to
wash around you, like music.
—Roald Dahl, *Matilda*

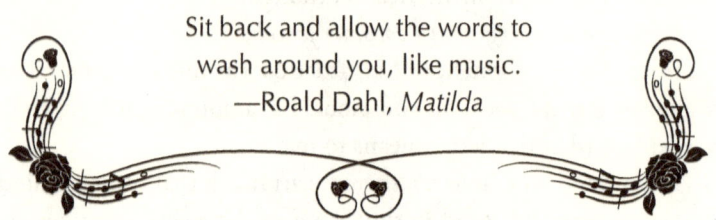

As soon as I sat down in that brown cushioned floor chair, staring into Jamuna's eyes, I was overcome with a million emotions. I had always been one to avoid direct eye contact. And being in that chair, knowing I would be directly confronted with all my shadows, knowing that I would be *seen* … it was a lot to take in. My muscles tensed up as if I was being electrified.

I was currently on the floor of a living room in a retreat house in Temecula, California, surrounded by a circle of six women I'd met the day before.

The situation evolved quickly, so let me rewind a bit.

The week prior, I saw an ad on Instagram. *An inner child healing retreat. Go through the trauma informed process, and then learn how to facilitate it yourself. September 14th through the 17th.*

September. Septembers have been hard since I lost my mom.

It was about to be the fifth anniversary of my mom's death. The old feelings of sadness and fear were beginning to edge their way through my newfound conviction.

Maybe community is just what you need.

Okay voice. I won't argue with you. I signed up.

I had been excited about going through the inner child healing process all the way up to the night before.

Then I woke up the next day with the heaviness of grief on my heart, and became hyper aware of the fact that I was surrounded by complete strangers. I questioned if I had made the right decision by coming here.

But I *was* here. There was no turning back. So I sat on the floor pillow and stared into Jamuna's eyes. They were gentle, brightened by the wavy ginger hair framing her face.

That did nothing to calm my nerves. It felt like she was staring into my soul. I felt so exposed in the center of that circle.

"How do you feel?" Jamuna started.

"I feel like I can't breathe," I managed to get out. I closed my eyes.

"Do you feel a tightness or a heaviness in your chest?" she asked.

"Heaviness."

"Heaviness almost always means grief." A pause. "That makes sense."

After a few moments of silence she continued. "What do you feel grief about?"

It took me at least ten seconds to respond. It was hard to find words. It felt like I had lost the ability to speak.

"My mom," I eventually managed to choke out.

"Today's the anniversary of the day she passed, right?" Jamuna confirmed.

I nodded.

Then I quickly sidestepped the issue. "But I feel like I've done a lot of healing in that aspect recently. One of the things I can't seem to fix, though, is this deep-rooted feeling of unworthiness …"

I laugh looking back on it now. My brain was avoiding confronting the pain of grief at all costs, even if it meant diving headfirst into other difficult memories.

"When going through things in my childhood home, my dad found a bunch of old home movies. This past Christmas, he digitized them and sent the videos over to me and my sisters as a gift. I thought it would be hard to watch them back, to see my mom alive, and it was. But it was also really difficult for another reason I wasn't expecting. There were so many times I was excited about things, or trying to get people's attention, and no one would listen to me, or I would get dismissed …"

Maybe my family's energy and focus was used up by the time I came into the picture. Maybe my parents were better able to connect with my older sisters. Maybe three kids were too many. Maybe it didn't have anything to do with *me*.

But as my mind began drifting back through the old home movies, my entire body contorted with shame. A specific video came to mind. It was Father's Day, and my family was sitting in the living room. I was around three at the time.

One by one, my sisters walked up and gave Dad cards and presents and crafts they had made at school. He would make a big deal and start admiring the gift or reading the card together with them. I would run up to try to be included.

"Can I see, Daddy?"

I was ignored or only half acknowledged. As the minutes passed, I would cycle between trying to be seen, and then going off to the side and focusing on something else when I wasn't included.

Another present. "Let me see! Let me see!"

Dad said nothing, raised the card above my reaching hands, and continued his conversation with my mom about the card for the camera, as if I wasn't even there.

Mom asked me to move out of the way of the shot.

The camera zoomed in until the drawing on the front of the card filled the screen.

In the background you can hear me yelling, "Daddy! Daddy!

Daaaaaddy!"

My voice broke on the last cry. The camera zoomed out and the card was finally passed into my hands to look at.

No words. I wasn't directly addressed the whole time.

Nancy handed him another craft project. I reached out.

"Let me see, let me see," I started to say again.

"Just a minute," my dad snapped, raising the present above my head where I couldn't reach. He finished reading, and then passed it off without looking in my direction, turning to hug Nancy.

The first time I found that video, I couldn't watch it all the way through. The sharpness of my whiny kid tone cut through the air like a blade. "Let me see! Let me see!" My shoulders tensed up as I prayed I would turn to dust.

I was so *annoying*. Why couldn't I just *shut up*. That day wasn't about *me*.

But another part of me was saying, *Heather you were* three. *You weren't even old enough to know what being annoying meant. You were just trying to be* included.

Jamuna's voice cut through the memory. "What do you think little Heather needed in that moment?"

"To be seen."

I felt the pain so strongly. The pain of simply being who I was, trying to be involved, and being dismissed. Being *annoying*.

The Girl Who Ruined Father's Day.

"It was so hard to watch it back. Because I just saw myself continuously crying out for attention. Nobody fully saw me. I was only included as an afterthought. And as I watched, I couldn't stop cringing. I thought to myself, *Wow, I was SO annoying.* I was *such* a difficult child. My voice was so *whiny*. But then I tell myself I wasn't even old enough to know any better. To even know what being annoying *was*. I was *three*. I was so small. I was just being *myself*."

I cried. I felt hands on my back and shoulders, the supportive energy of the other women in the circle, urging me to keep going. It was comforting, and at the same time it was weird to feel held by anyone. I couldn't remember the last time I had been hugged.

Jamuna flipped the script. "You weren't annoying. You were using the way you knew how to get attention. Using your voice. Little you was *smart.*"

I smiled a bit through the tears. I had never thought about it that way before. Little me *was* smart, using her voice to garner attention.

"And determined," I added with a laugh. "She wouldn't stop until she got what she wanted."

Jamuna nodded. "Just because she didn't get that attention, doesn't mean she didn't deserve it."

That phrase reverberated in my ears.

It doesn't mean I didn't deserve it.

I want to pause to be really clear once again. I *love* my parents and I *know* they loved me. I don't believe they were ever *intentionally* ignoring me.

There were a lot of positive memories in those movies as well. My parents were doing their best. But I was also the *third* child. My parents already had a lot on their plate. And so I think, sometimes, I felt the ramifications of that.

I held so much *shame* for being too much.

Another voice came from behind me. It was Chassie, one of the other women attending the retreat.

"I just want to let you know that I feel her right now. Your Mom is here with you."

I opened my eyes to look back in her direction. Her blond hair fell in front of her face, half shielding her eyes, but I could see that they were brimming with emotion. After a moment, she spoke again.

"She wants you to say her name."

I froze.

Chassie was *channeling my mom.*

I hadn't said Mom's name since that one night in my apartment, and it felt just as difficult as it was then.

Finally, I forced it out, the sound feeling foreign in my throat. "Laura."

"She wants you to talk about her," Chassie continued.

I took a deep breath.

Then it all came spilling out.

"She was the most kind and loving and selfless person I've ever met," I started. "I know our relationship wasn't perfect, and we had fights sometimes when I was a teenager, but I always knew she was trying to do what she thought was best for me."

I smiled as memories I hadn't thought of in a long time came flooding back to the surface. "She loved the beach, and the ocean, and her favorite movie was *Dirty Dancing*. It's funny because I didn't watch the full movie until after she passed, and when I did, I was like *Mommmm,* because that movie is all about being carefree, risky, and rebellious. And about a woman stepping into her sensuality and authentic expression."

"I'm not sure why, I wish I could ask her, but growing up she would give me and my sisters music boxes. Every holiday or birthday we would get one. And every night, at least up until high school, she would come upstairs to say goodnight. She would ask which music box we wanted to hear. She would turn the dial, the music would start playing, and she would sit with us until it ended. Then she would kiss us goodnight and leave the room."

I began to cry again. "The day my mom had her stroke was the day she moved me into college. I got the call while at the opening ceremony. When I got back to my dorm later that night, there was a gift bag sitting on my desk, along with a letter. That letter ended up being the last thing she ever wrote."

"I was rereading that letter this morning, and one of the things it said was, *It seems like only yesterday you were running around the playground at the Rez, making friends with everyone you met.* I feel like that version of me, the carefree, bubbly girl that my mom saw me as, that was who I truly was, and I just lost touch with that part of myself as I grew up."

Chassie spoke again. I could tell from the sound of her voice that she was crying too.

"She's saying it's okay for you to sing, and to dance, and to play, and to find joy."

Even more tears welled up in my eyes and I couldn't stop them from spilling over.

"She wants you to know that just because she died, doesn't mean the music stopped playing."

I exhaled, and it felt like I was releasing a breath I had been holding onto for five long years. The heaviness I had held when I sat down in that chair began to dissipate.

Because it seemed like once Mom was gone, the music, the magic, the joy, the love in my life was gone too. I didn't think I'd ever get it back again.

And a part of me felt guilty for even trying to. Like I could never truly feel happiness again without her here, or I would be dishonoring her memory.

But here Mom was, giving me permission to keep living on without her. To find joy again. To listen for the music.

Slowly, the corners of my mouth began to turn upward. I don't think I can fully put into words what I felt in that moment. Like a five-year weight was lifted off my chest.

After a moment, Chassie laughed, "She's saying she is Baby."

Baby, the main character from *Dirty Dancing*.

I laughed with her. "Like she's saying that I am Baby? Or that my mom is Baby?"

"Your mom is Baby," Chassie clarified. "She's saying that that rebellious, free spirit of Baby, that was the version of herself that she loved the most. It is who she is now. And she is happy now and at total peace with what happened."

After my session ended, I took a walk in the woods behind the retreat house to clear my head.

What an overwhelming and powerful experience.

I walked the path, climbing further up the hill, surrounded by trees and enveloped in silence, lost in my own thoughts.

Through the trees I heard the soft pinging of a melody. It was a wind chime, blowing somewhere off in the distance.

The music never stopped playing.

My Own Little Corner

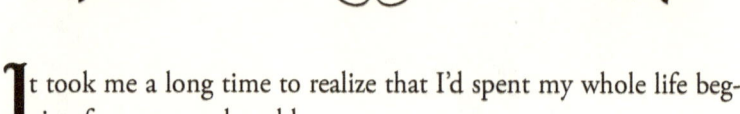

*It's amazing how close you are to
your essential self as a kid, he thought,
and how far from it you drift the more
you strive to be loved.*
—Nina George, *The Little Paris Bookshop*

It took me a long time to realize that I'd spent my whole life begging for a seat at the table.

Literally.

Growing up, there was my mom and dad, my two sisters—Jenny and Nancy—and me—the youngest. My family lived in a white house with rust accents, perched at the top of a hill. We had a fairly small kitchen laid with burnt red countertops. There was an island in the center with a slightly lower surface jutting out of it on one side, creating a three-sided table. It was just big enough to fit one chair on either short side, and two chairs on the long side. Dad, Jenny, Nancy, Mom.

Four seats at the table.

Then I came along and disrupted everything—it's what I'm known for. A haphazard solution emerged. One of those small two-step stools with a padded top and a metal bar that dug into my back, situated at the corner between Nancy and Mom.

Right behind the padded vinyl material of the seat was a small tab. If you pulled it up, the stepstool folded flat, conveniently fitting back into the closet until the next time it was needed.

"Dinner time!" Stool comes out.

Dinner's over. Stool goes back.

This was not a short-term solution to handle small rambunctious children. Only after my eldest sister went off to college did I graduate to a big girl chair.

I was thirteen. I should've gotten a cake.

Looking back on it now, I can't help but think that over time, I *became* that stepstool. Molding myself into spaces I no longer fit … flattening myself for convenience … not daring to take up space. The table was meant for four chairs, and I will always be the fifth.

Ten steps from the kitchen was a long, wooden table. Six wooden chairs sat around it.

Our dining room. I can still envision it now.

Is this where it started? Is this where I began to learn that I wasn't enough?

Because we *had* a bigger table. We *had* a table where I could have a real chair. Where everyone could be equals. And we didn't use it.

I wasn't *worth* the ten steps.

I get it. Carrying the dishes a little farther to the sink is a hassle. And I didn't want to cause a fuss.

But maybe it would've been nice if someone did.

I *know* my parents loved me. I *know* it wasn't intentional. I *know* if my mom knew how I felt about it now, she would've brought us to the dining room immediately. I grieve the loss of the ability for us to have a conversation about it.

And now as an adult, I can look at the situation and see that it was just about convenience. Unfortunately, *kid brains don't think that way.*

All Elementary School Heather knew was that she was always relegated to the corner of the table. Then she would go to school, sitting in classrooms where she was constantly the odd one out, the last one picked, the one left standing on the sidelines of the playground. And those were the two main events of her small life. School—excluded. Home—corner of the table. Over time, this became a dangerous feedback loop, each experience more fuel to shape her negative perception of the other.

It was a new day in the magical retreat house in the mountains of Temecula. Two days ago we were a group of seven strangers, but now we had witnessed each other in some of our deepest pain.

And it wasn't over. Today we were going to learn how to facilitate the healing process ourselves, and then practice on each other.

That meant I had to go back in the hot seat again.

This time I was paired with a woman named Jillian. She had auburn hair and one of the warmest smiles I've ever encountered.

I closed my eyes and set my intention.

"I feel like I really want to let go of this deep-rooted feeling of unworthiness."

"Are there any memories from childhood that bring that up for you?" Jillian asked.

I took a deep breath and told her about the stepstool.

But I started to dismiss myself. "I know it seems like not that big of a deal, but I was so little when it began, and it lasted such a long time. I think it had a deep effect on me."

"Can you see the kitchen right now?"

"Yes," I breathed out.

There I was, my twenty-three-year-old self, standing in that small kitchen. It had been a long time since I had been here. I glanced from the rust-red counter, to my dad and mom sitting across from each other, to my sisters sitting in their chairs on the long side, and finally to little Heather at the corner, smiling and bouncing up and down on her little stepstool. Tears began welling up in my eyes. She deserved better.

"What would you say to little Heather?" Jillian asked me.

I replied with no hesitation. "That she deserves a seat at the table."

Jillian guided me further. "Well why don't we give her a seat. Imagine little Heather has her own chair at the table now. How does she feel?"

I breathed in slowly, and imagined little Heather in a brown, wooden chair like the others.

But Heather's a little too short. She's probably struggling a bit to reach her plate, and thinking that the wood of the seat is a little too hard …

I laughed at the fact that she still wasn't satisfied.

"I think she needs a cushion," I challenged, stifling a giggle.

Jillian chuckled. "Well, then why don't we give her that cushion."

So I gave her a cushion. A big, soft, royal blue one.

I looked down at her small face again. Now she was beaming from ear to ear, sitting comfortably, and fully able to reach her fork and her plate.

Once I made sure that little Heather felt happy and fulfilled in that memory—and had finished eating her dinner—Jillian had me bring her back with me to my safe place, a secluded beach by the ocean.

"How does little Heather feel now?" Jillian asked.

I smiled. "She feels great. She's got a beach chair."

When I was first sitting in my chair in that memory, I had wondered whether or not I should tell Jillian that little Heather wanted a cushion.

But I'm glad that I did. The cushion was an important symbol.

I had spent my entire life scared to speak up for myself. Even when I tried, I was misunderstood or silenced by other people. So I never voiced what I needed, let alone what I *wanted*.

But now I know what I need. And I know what I deserve. And it's more than the bare minimum.

I deserve the chair *and* a goddamn cushion.

And thanks to Jillian, now I know that I can give it to myself. I know that whenever I am struggling, I can always close my eyes and give little Heather her cushion.

REST IN PEACE

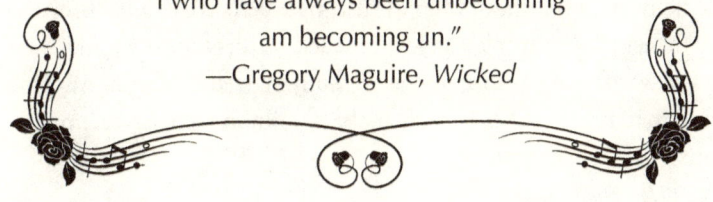

"It's unbecoming," she agreed. "A perfect
word for my new life. Unbecoming.
I who have always been unbecoming
am becoming un."
—Gregory Maguire, *Wicked*

Later that night, the other women and I sat down in the living
room of the retreat house, on top of small mattress cushions
laid out on the floor.

A woman sat in front of us, surrounded by seven crystal bowls of
various sizes—one for each of the seven chakras. She introduced herself as Jess. Jess had wavy chestnut hair and kind eyes. She would be
taking us through a round of breathwork followed by sound healing.

I was immediately captivated by her energy. It felt safe.

I sat up straight and looked toward the front of the room like
an eager kindergarten student. I had no idea what to expect—I had
never done breathwork before—but it sounded cool. I was excited.

We began by going around the room and setting intentions—
something we wanted to expand into and something we wanted to
release.

I already knew my answer. My intention had been the same
throughout the weekend. I wanted to expand my voice and presence,
because I knew I had valuable things to say and teach and share, if
only I could learn to unapologetically take up space. And I wanted

to *finally* release this intense feeling of unworthiness, that I am undeserving, and this fear of being seen, so that I could fully step into my purpose and begin to serve others.

Jess advised me to make myself as big as possible, to teach my body to take up more space. I giggled and spread my legs and arms out wide as we laid down on our cushions. I was going full starfish mode.

We started a rhythmic pattern of rapid breathing. Breathe into the belly, then the chest, then breathe out. *Belly, chest, out. Belly, chest, out.* Music began to play as Jess coached us through the journey.

It wasn't long before my entire body started to tingle. And soon after that my mind began to make a million excuses to not keep going.

Belly, chest, out.

How long are we going to do this?

Belly, chest, out.

You're thirsty, get up and go drink water.

Belly, chest, out.

You're tired, just start breathing normally again.

I tuned that voice out and focused on my breath. Listening to my internal voice of fear had gotten me nowhere in life. And I was starting to learn the importance of *keeping my word.*

I was not going to quit.

The music crescendoed, and the tingling feelings in my body started getting more and more intense. I felt fuzzy—fuzzy like when you're sitting for too long and your foot falls asleep, fuzzy like seeing the black and white static buzzing on an old TV.

Jess began to give us affirmations to repeat out loud.

"I am a gift," she said.

"I am a gift," I repeated—although I think my mousy tone was a dead giveaway that I felt less than birthday ready in that moment.

"I am free to step into my purpose."

"I am free to step into my purpose."

I was a little louder this time. I tried to put a little more intention and emphasis behind my words.

"I deserve to have a voice."

"I *deserve* to have a *voice*."

I said those last words with a conviction and a power that felt foreign on my tongue. I shocked myself in that moment—I didn't recognize my own voice when it wasn't timid or small.

The music got even louder. *Belly, chest, out. Belly, chest, out.* I could occasionally hear crying from the other women. This, along with the music, Jess' voice, and the sharp intakes and outtakes of breath, combined to make a dramatic symphony of pain and release.

I suddenly became aware of my hands. I was so caught up in my mind that I had temporarily forgotten about my body. They were not spread out on the ground anymore; I was no longer a starfish. Instead, my forearms were lifted off the ground and stationed in front of my face—my hands contorted and wrapped so tightly they resembled lobster claws.

Jess had warned us about this beforehand. Scientifically, hand cramping—or tetany—can mean that you have lower CO_2 levels in your body, which can result from exhaling more than you inhale. Spiritually, however, it can mean you are having a hard time letting go of something.

My hands were not just intricately wrapped claws though. They were also immobile. I kept sending signals from my brain, yelling at my hands, *Move! Move!*

Not an inch.

My hands would not listen to me. My forearms wouldn't either. I was stuck in the t-rex arm position. A calcified fossil. Attempting to move resulted in a slight tremor at the tips of my fingers, and nothing more.

My thought process went like this: *This is absolutely terrifying, to lose control of my body …*

Then another voice chimed in.

But you already lost control, Heather. It didn't start right now. As you grew up more and more isolated and outcasted, you started to lose sight of who you were, in the quest for approval from other people. And after Mom's death, it just spiraled more and more out of control. The past took hold of your brain, and you were living in survival mode. You woke up one day and you were somebody you didn't recognize.

I began sobbing. Grief hit me like a wave. But this time I wasn't grieving the loss of my mom.

I was grieving the loss of myself.

I felt like me in my truest form was the way Mom wrote about me in her letter, *at the Rez, making friends with everyone you met.* And somewhere along the way I lost her.

I stopped dancing. I stopped hearing the music. I lost Heather.

By this point we had switched back to normal breathing and Jess had begun the sound healing with the crystal chakra bowls. As the magical tones vibrated through the air, I was still lying there, crying, with my t-rex lobster hands contorted above my head.

They felt like chains. Inside my hands was all my trauma, all my negative beliefs that I had not been able to let go of. I felt imprisoned by my own mind.

The more I realized how long these chains had been bound to me, the harder the tears fell.

A sentiment I had kept saying in the past few months was that it felt like I was only just now starting to live. And while releasing the past and experiencing life in a new and youthful way is beautiful, it also meant mourning everything that came before. It meant mourning all the years that I had been asleep at the wheel. Knowing that all those years spent living in survival mode molded me into who I am today, yet knowing it is time that I will never get back.

Slowly but surely, my hands began to unfurl. Tears streamed relentlessly down my face. As I laid there with the pulsing sound of the chakra bowl in the background, it felt like I was holding a funeral for myself.

This is where I finally lay Trauma Heather to rest. She is dead now.

But from her ashes comes the true Heather. The one I always was at my core. The one who was a light to other people. The one who brought people together, the way my mom saw me.

And she is even stronger now. Because she has been through hell and back again. And if that couldn't dim her fire, then nothing can.

I had started to resonate with the image of the phoenix.

I am rising.

WELCOME HOME, DAUGHTER

"I'm just trying to get home," said Heather.
But she was already home. That was
the point, entirely.
—Jean Hanff Korelitz, *The Sabbathday River*

My weekend in Temecula was so transformative that I returned to my San Diego apartment fully expecting to embody this new me that I thought I had become.

That was not the case.

I was thrust back into my old environment. The same streets. The same patterns. The same heavy energy. It was overwhelming.

Being in nature, in such a healing space, just made it painstakingly obvious upon my return that the energy of being in a city, surrounded by so many people—and so many unconscious people—was too much for me to handle. I looked around at my apartment, the one that two months ago I thought was my dream, and it started to feel like a prison. I needed to be in a forest or a jungle somewhere, not sitting in a box on a grid, paying gas and electric and looking for street parking.

I also began feeling this deep call to travel. It was not a new feeling. It was one I had felt during college, but COVID had interrupted my plans. Then in April of 2023, I had the opportunity to go to Morocco and film with local cooperatives.

I still remember how shocked I was in that foreign place, to learn that schedules and work *always* took a backseat to teatime. We would enter a cooperative, camera gear at the ready, and immediately be offered the opportunity to sit and have tea. Backpacks and tripods would be forgotten near the door, and cups passed around the table. I would slowly savor the taste of a date I was munching on, all the while musing about how backwards it felt, to focus on being, *before* doing.

In the past I had been blinded, stuck in my own cultural bubble. I think that trip was the first time that I opened my eyes to the fact that the society in which I had been living was not the only one out there. I was in awe of how open, warm, and hospitable the Moroccan people were. They had a simpler way of living, one which made space for generosity and humanity.

Something America could use a whole lot more of.

When my plane landed back in the US, people impatiently made their way off the plane, with no regard for the people surrounding them. I stood on the sidelines of the baggage claim as they swarmed to the beginning of the belt, trying to grab their bag first. People stared at their screens. A crowd, but only in name. People didn't see or acknowledge one another. It was all so *individual*.

I quickened my pace. It felt like the walls were slowly closing in on me, even as I walked through the JFK terminal with its high ceilings soaring above.

We have made our world too complex here. It distances us from ourselves.

In Temecula, I had gotten a taste of humanity again. Of genuine human interaction. And then I came back to San Diego, once again feeling like I couldn't breathe. It was as if I was living in a different reality from everyone else. I felt lonelier in a crowd than by myself. I spent days alone in my apartment, or walking along the ocean, stuck in my mind.

I kept thinking to myself, *Why am I here? I don't belong here.* I was beginning to build my business remotely, but I wasn't making income yet. And I was paying city prices to live in a city, when all I wanted to do was disappear into nature.

Should I leave?

I sat in my blue papasan chair, looking around at my apartment, when realization dawned on me. I gasped and pulled out my phone, scrolling all the way down on my Instagram profile to a post I had put out four months prior, on my birthday.

Twenty-three things I learned at twenty-three. This was number twenty:

Stay in touch with your values, and make sure your spending aligns with those values. For example, I don't need a nice apartment, I would rather save on rent and use my money to travel.

And yet, here I was, sitting in my nice apartment—a blatant hypocrite.

I was in the apartment I said I *didn't* need. I realized that I had been living passively, just taking the next step and next step in front of me. I had lost touch with my own values. I was living out of alignment with myself and what I wanted.

I was living someone else's dream. It wasn't mine.

The call to leave grew louder.

The next morning, I journaled about this. Since the end of August, I had been doing stream-of-consciousness journaling every morning, taking the advice of Julia Cameron in *The Artist's Way: A Spiritual Path to Higher Creativity.*

This has been an invaluable practice. I have an entire document of my thoughts and the rapid mindset shifts I have undergone during my awakening.

But on this day it became more than that.

It started off like any other journaling session. Writing whatever came to mind. And as I looked at the apartment around me, filled with stuff, what was coming to mind was that I had to leave.

I *knew* I had to leave. But it felt so overwhelming. I didn't know where to start. I began having a battle within myself, listing out what I would need to do to prepare, while simultaneously wondering how I would ever have the strength to leave the life that I knew.

Then something shifted. The longer I had been writing, the more stream of consciousness the words became. I felt my conscious brain slipping slowly, further and further back into the recesses of my mind. It was like I became the passenger in my own car, as my hand was still writing and words were still coming into my head.

But they weren't my words.

The quality of my handwriting changed as I continued writing, almost semi-conscious, eyes half rolled back into my head:

Heather, I know it's scary but you KNOW you need to leave. You KNOW you aren't meant to be here. You KNOW this is your dream and this is what you need to do to get it. Your new life will cost you your old one, your new life will cost you your old one. Do you want things or do you want fulfillment? Do you want comfortable and regrets or freedom? You know what you need to do, you know what you need to do. Start preparing, you need to prepare, you know what's coming, you know it's coming, it's almost here. You need to be ready, you need to be ready, you need to prepare. Let go let go let go, you know you have to let go, remember your claw hands? You have to let go of the chains that bind you. Your environment is depleting your energy. Cleanse, cleanse, prepare, your time is coming and you need to be ready. It will be unexpected, your life will be unrecognizable, but you have to take the leap. We want to give you what you want, we want to give you what you want. Do you want it? Do you really want it? We need proof. This is it, commit yourself, unlock the fire within you. No longer time to stay comfortable. It's go time, girl. Go time. Go time. Go time.

My normal brain came online again for half a second, as I tried to make sense of what was happening.

Oh my god! Why is this pull so strong? I'm losing my mind, but I'll also lose my mind if I don't go. I have to get out. I have to ...

Then this unseen force took back control over my mind and continued its preaching:

Heather, you can do this. Do you hear the siren call? Follow the call, follow the music, I am guiding you, follow my voice. I have the answers, I have the answers, and I want to give them to you, let me. Follow the path, follow your instructions, all will be revealed in time Heather, in time. Have faith, I love you so much, this is your call. One step, you don't need the plan, just one step, one step. We have the map. We will guide you. Let us do it. Stop resisting. Stop resisting. You know what you need to do.

Finally, I finished writing, my normal brain came fully back online, and I set my journal down on the table and looked at the pages.

What the fuck was that?

I put my head in my hands and stared at the page.

I had written an *entire* message. Pages full of words that *weren't my words*, my brain full of thoughts that *weren't my thoughts*.

I learned later that I had accidentally stumbled upon the practice of channeled writing.

But in that moment, it was an intense message. I was immediately very overwhelmed. I didn't know what to do about it. And I had a coaching call scheduled that morning with Kai, so I put my journal away and ignored it.

A few hours later, the memory of my cryptic message came flooding back. I pulled my journal out and reread the words.

I need to leave? I need to get rid of my stuff and take off into the unknown? Was I ready for that?

I stared at the frantic scribbles of ink on the page until all the words began to blend together. I was so scared.

But as I scanned the message, I knew that that last paragraph was my mom speaking to me.

Follow the music, follow my voice.

I am always listening to music, and this moment was no exception. As I continued reading the message in fear, a new song came on. One I had never heard before.

It began with the soft whoosh of a rushing breeze, and then slowly, the sound of wind chimes creeped in.

Mom?

The song was called "Welcome Home, Son" by Radical Face. The chimes faded into words as the song reached its chorus and the guitar and piano chords swelled.

I stared at the title *Welcome Home* written on my phone screen. Then I looked back at the pages telling me to leave.

I started sobbing. I was so scared to leave my apartment. But even though I felt like I couldn't leave, it didn't feel like home to me.

What *is* home?

As the voices continued crooning, and wind chimes fluttered in throughout the bridge, that question just played over and over again in my mind.

What is home? What is home? What is home?

I had lived in the same house from the time I was born, to when

I was eighteen. 184 Pine Hill Road. *That* was home to me.

But then I went to college. And my mom passed. On breaks I would return back to the same address. But she wasn't there.

It wasn't home anymore. It was an empty house.

Then COVID hit and that house was sold. I bounced from home to home. *Other* people's homes. I had moved *seven* times in just over three years.

In and out, in and out, in and out. Displaced and settled and displaced again. I realized that even when I had gotten this apartment, the freedom was nice, but it didn't feel like home. Because *nothing ever did.*

But *Welcome Home* the song title beckoned. I buried my face in my hands as the wind chimes reverberated in my ears. I had put the song on repeat, as I often do when one speaks to me.

Welcome home? But the message was telling me to leave.

What is home? What is home? What is home?

I slowly raised my head as it dawned on me, the lesson I needed to learn to follow this call.

In the past five years, I had been looking for home *outside of myself,* always feeling displaced and disappointed.

But *what is home?* Home is safety, home is security.

I needed to cultivate that within *myself.*

I needed to make *myself* my home. Make myself feel safe within my body and mind.

Then, I could be at home anywhere I am. Because I know that *nothing* in the external world is promised.

I am listening, Mom. I am following the music.

I Am Baby

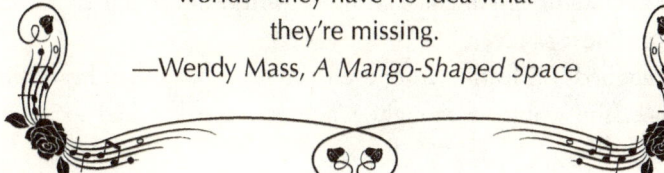

All those people in their black-and-white
worlds—they have no idea what
they're missing.
—Wendy Mass, *A Mango-Shaped Space*

A few days later, the sky was losing its light as I stepped into a small storefront. The magic possibilities of evening electrified the air. There was a woman standing at a table in front of me.

"What are your intentions for tonight?" she asked.

"To let go of the past and live in the present in order to move toward my future," I declared.

She smiled and beckoned me into the room behind her.

Three days prior, I had told my friend how reigniting my love for dance had been significant in my healing. Closing my eyes and moving my body to music allowed me to begin to move through all the emotions that had been sitting stagnant, stuck in my body for years.

She suggested I go to something called ecstatic dance. She thought I would like it.

I had never heard of it, but I decided I'll try almost anything once. The very next day, I was walking past a store when a flier caught my eye. *Ecstatic dance. This Friday night!*

As you and I both know by now, there are no coincidences, so I went home and purchased a ticket online. Two days later, I was wearing flowy pants in an open room surrounded by strangers, with no idea what to expect.

Around fifty people sat in a circle. In the front center of the room was a DJ booth with an altar in front of it, covered in leaves and candles.

To open the space, we passed a rose around the circle, sharing with our neighbor something we were grateful for as we did.

"I'm grateful for guidance from my spirit team," I said as I turned to the girl next to me.

I laughed. If Heather from even *two months* ago had heard that sentence, she would've thought whoever uttered it had lost their mind.

And now here we were. I guess I had to lose my mind to find myself.

We began with some ice breakers—I'd imagine some breaking of the ice was necessary to fully express yourself through dance in front of strangers.

A woman stood at the front of the room and asked us to start walking around the space.

After some time had passed, she told us to stop in front of the next person we made eye contact with. My eyes' attention was quickly taken by a pair of chocolate hazel eyes. Their owner was a short Asian woman, with shoulder-length, wavy black hair. She wore a red tank-top bodysuit, ending at the thigh, with cutouts around the midsection. A golden chain came down from her neck and wrapped around her waist. Her warmth was palpable and mesmerizing.

Through the speakers came our next instructions. We were to stare into our partner's eyes and not say a word.

I've always avoided eye contact as much as possible. It made me uncomfortable. Eyes were lasers, beaming through my skull and leaving irreparable damage. I've always said direct eye contact felt like people were staring into my soul. And so my direct, sustained eye contact had been reserved only for past lovers. Having a stranger stare into my soul was a new level of vulnerability I didn't know if my self-concept could take.

But now, I was in front of this woman. What was I going to do? Tap out just because I couldn't handle a staring contest?

I endured.

The first minute was an exchange of smiles and giggles as this woman and I navigated the unfamiliar intimacy of this moment. Then I suppressed my laughter and attempted to get lost in her eyes.

How odd, I found myself thinking. All the humans we interact with, the friends we have, the people we pass on the street, and yet how many of them do we take the time to really get to know? To really *see*. On a *soul* level. Past the menial day to day, the trivial grievances, the occupation, the dress, the appearance.

I felt like there were very few people in this world I had taken the time to truly see, at least until I had left my job and started paying attention to the world around me. For so long, assumptions, preconceived notions, and categories had created an illusion of the person in front of me, clouding their soul.

After maybe three minutes, we were advised to move on without a word. How odd to have such an intimate moment with a stranger and to not even get their name, not even hear their voice.

The next time we walked around the room, we stopped and made a group of four. One by one, we were to stand in the center of our small circle and dance to the music. The people on the outside of the circle would watch, and when they saw a part of our body that was tense, they were to touch it. This way, we would become more aware of our bodies and where we needed to let loose.

Dancing directly in front of three strangers and letting them touch you? I did *not* realize this was going to be part of the agenda. Anxiety I had not felt in months crept back in, and I nervously waited until I was the last to go.

Eventually my turn came, and I could avoid it no longer. I closed my eyes as the music started playing, and hesitantly began to move my body. I tried to make my movements light and airy, but I felt a bit like the wacky inflatable tube man you see outside a car wash.

I felt a hand on my neck. My entire head had been locked—I hadn't even noticed.

I leaned back into a head roll. Then I felt a hand on my hips—I hadn't realized I wasn't using them either. I started to move my hips back and forth, isolating them from my core to create more fluid movement.

By the time the music stopped, I felt like I had uncovered parts of my body I hadn't used in years.

Or possibly ever.

After the end of the unusual ice breakers, we all sat in a circle for a performance. A woman glided toward the center of the room with two torches, one in each hand. As music began to play over the speakers, she danced and spun the torches, playing with fire.

I was mesmerized—but not just because this woman was spinning fire around her head. She was moving with a fluidity, a sensuality, and a presence that one does not find easily these days. To be so in touch with her body, her powerful femininity, in front of a group of strangers … I was envious of her. I wanted that for myself. My mind had always held me back.

Watching her was like being in a trance. I didn't want it to end. But eventually she blew the fire out and took her final bow.

Now it was time to really dance.

We all sat down on the floor with our eyes closed. Then the music began to play. Guided by a woman's voice, slowly, we began to crawl. Then, we began rising to our feet. And then all bets were off.

I looked around and saw people shaking, spinning, waving their arms, some were on the floor, some standing—all varieties of expression were present. It was unlike anything I had ever seen before.

I closed my eyes and attempted to feel the music, moving in the way my body wanted to, without my mind jumping in to say *that looks stupid!* The less I thought, the freer my movement became.

There was a lightness in my body I'm not sure I had ever felt before. I rolled my head and swayed my hips, remembering my instructions from earlier.

Soon enough, all tension was gone from my muscles, all thoughts gone from my head. I spun and floated across the floor and through the other dancers, without any notion of what I looked like or what others were doing. I was completely present in my body, and completely shut off from my mind.

It was pure liberation.

I stayed in this otherworldly realm for an hour or two. I didn't want to stop moving, but eventually I needed to catch my breath. I walked off the dance floor and sat on a couch in the corner of the room.

I started observing the other dancers I had just walked away from. I was now on the outside, looking in, and I began to remember how uncommon and unorthodox this type of event was. I watched the dancers as if watching lions at the zoo.

Then I realized something. My mouth fell open as goosebumps raised on my arms.

I was living in a scene out of Dirty Dancing.

The one near the beginning of the film. Where Baby walks into the workers' lounge with a watermelon, and is confronted with a world she's never seen before. Raw, sensual, human expression.

Dirty Dancing.

It is in this scene that she dances with Johnny and for the first time, gets a taste of how it feels to stop moving through life so tightly wound.

Well tonight, *I* was Baby.

I came into this space carrying my giant watermelon of burdens. But I laid them at the door, and soon became completely enraptured by this world that was so beyond the limits of what I used to think life was.

I began to truly dance like no one was watching, and in dancing,

I found ultimate freedom.

The corners of my mouth stretched upward as if they would never be pulled back down again. I couldn't stop the smile from overtaking my face.

After hearing Chassie's channeled message back in Temecula, I had wanted to start walking in Mom's footsteps by becoming more like Baby. But I didn't realize that I was going to actually *become Baby*.

It was such a beautiful, indescribable, full-circle moment.

And I know Mom planned it perfectly, just for me.

THE SIREN CALL

Before I got here, I thought for a long time
that the way out of the labyrinth was to
pretend that it did not exist, to build a small,
self-sufficient world in a back corner of the
endless maze and to pretend that I was not
lost, but home. But that only led to a lonely
life accompanied only by the last words
of the already-dead …
—John Green, *Looking for Alaska*

I sashayed through the room of dancers and out into the courtyard. Nestled on a blanket, under a tree, lay a spread of oracle cards. I stared out at the dozens of cards and picked one that felt like it was calling out to me. I flipped it over.

#44 The Sacrifice.

Illustrated on the card was a beautiful woman cloaked in wisps of different colors. She had feathers fanning out from either side of her face, creating an elaborate looking headdress. She was looking up and one of her arms was outstretched toward the sky, with thin black designs trailing up her arm. Right above her open palm was a golden butterfly.

It was a beautiful card. I was mesmerized. I flipped open the oracle book to see what it said about it.

The book described how sacrifices are used as offerings to the gods to have their blessings magnified. The card called on the reader to take stock of the things they are clinging onto too tightly, and to offer them up to the universe to make space for new blessings.

What was the one thing I held closest to me? What was the one thing I felt I would not be able to live without?

Hmm. Interesting.

I went back to the dance floor and continued floating through the air.

The next morning, I woke up and immediately sat down for my meditation practice.

Deep breath in, deep breath out. Relax the body. Empty the mind. I slowly rolled my eyes up toward my third eye.

After about five or ten minutes of stillness, a song began playing in my head. It was one I had heard before. "Rabbit Heart (Raise It Up)" by Florence + The Machine.

I remember feeling joy when I first found that song a few months back, because in the lyrics she sings about a girl with a rabbit heart, and that made me think of Mom. Her favorite animal was a bunny.

You know those songs you know the words to and you sing along, but somehow your mind never takes the step to actually consciously *listen* and realize the message in the lyrics?

This was one of those times. I knew the lyrics to this song, but I had always sung it absentmindedly. Suddenly in meditation, a specific part of the song started playing in my head, and for the first time, I actually absorbed the lyrics and what they were saying.

They spoke of a scared girl with the heart of a rabbit. She needed to become brave, with the heart of a lion, before she would be able to offer up her last sacrifice.

I stayed on the floor as I contemplated my musical message.

The last sacrifice.

The oracle card from the night before had said that I needed to offer up to the universe the one thing I thought I could not live without, to make space for new blessings.

But this season was already full of so much purging, so much death, so much letting go of my old life.

What did I have left to give?

I knew.

Home. The physical one.

It was my apartment. The reason I was sobbing when I first read that channeled message, telling me to leave, was because I was absolutely terrified of letting go of comfort, stability, and the material.

And that was *exactly* why it had to be my sacrifice.

I had said I wanted to travel, and I couldn't have everything. I had to let go in order to receive. I had to build my home within myself.

I ended my meditation and looked across the room at the growing pile of stuff I had created to sell, ever since meeting that old man on his porch and talking about what really matters in life.

It began to feel like I was building an altar. An offering.

Not enough, but a start. I had to work my way up to the final offering. Become the lion-hearted girl first.

A Rabbit-Hearted
Garage Sale

That's what alchemists do. They show that,
when we strive to become better than we are,
everything around us becomes better, too.
—Paulo Coelho, *The Alchemist*

As clear as that journal message was about what I needed to do, I was overwhelmed. I was just the girl with a rabbit heart. *Get rid of 90 percent of what I own and hop on a plane to a foreign country by myself?* The more I thought about it, the more paralyzed I became.

But the end of the message fluttered back into my mind.

You don't need the plan, just one step, one step. We have the map. We will guide you. Let us do it. Stop resisting. Stop resisting. You know what you need to do.

My angels said I just needed to prepare. Put one foot in front of the other. So I stopped freaking myself out by looking at the big picture, and instead focused on baby steps. Normally if people are planning a trip, they book the ticket, and then get ready. Instead, I worked backward, because part of me still didn't believe I would ever get to the end result.

If I was going to leave, that meant there was a ton of stuff I needed to get rid of. No need to focus on a plane ticket right now. I needed to have a garage sale. Baby steps.

This was an impulsive garage sale. I had been scared into inaction by my journal message the entire week. Then one Friday night, I decided all my stuff needed to go. I threw more things into the center of the room and posted a Facebook ad for the very next morning.

I was worried no one would show up. I hadn't done any promotion besides the one post, just twelve hours before the start of the sale. So that night, I sat on my couch, looked up to the ceiling, and I prayed.

"Angels, Mom, I'm listening to you. I'm doing my part. I'm preparing. Can you help me out on your end? Please send the right people to my garage sale. Please send people to take some of these things so that I may be lighter."

I took one last glance over at the ever-growing pile of junk in the center of my apartment, and then went to sleep.

The morning started off well enough. I had one or two families come by right at the dot of 8:00 a.m. As the hour dragged on, a slow but steady trickle of people came through.

But these weren't just any ordinary people. The more I interacted with the attendees of my garage sale, the more I realized that all of them were heaven sent.

It started off with a lovely woman. She had an eccentric air about her, gray hair, and a purple sun hat. She noticed my book on the table, *Breath* by James Nestor. She asked me how it was, and described how she's felt like she's had this inability to breathe fully for as long as she could remember. I told her about how transformative breathwork had been for me. She left, resolved to go try it for herself.

A little later a young man came in. He was interested in my two small jars of paint. He talked about how he used to be a painter and had lost his drive for creativity over the years. He was hoping these paints would help him ease back into it. I showed him a little portable easel I had as well, gave him some words of encouragement, and he left, resolved to resume his artistic pursuits he had left by the wayside for too long.

The next man to come in was older, and also an artist. Although this time, I was the one being given the pep talk. He noticed the small sign I had painted, sitting up against a wall, and asked if I was an artist. I begrudgingly said that I was, but I had a deep creative block that I was trying to work through. He began telling me about his own artistic journey, the galleries he had been in, and pulled out his phone to show me some of his work.

As he swiped through photos on his camera roll, he turned toward me. "I'm showing this to you because I want to inspire you to reconnect with your art again," he said.

I felt my insides go warm and I smiled at the fact that this man I had just met cared this much about helping reignite my creativity.

After showing me his work, he noticed the giant swallowtail butterfly I had on my desk. A real one, flattened within a frame. I had purchased it at another garage sale about a month before.

The man said that just yesterday, he had witnessed two giant swallowtail butterflies sitting outside his apartment, flapping their wings in a mating dance for hours. He showed me a video he had taken on his phone of the scene.

I peered closer at the phone to see two butterflies sitting on the concrete, whirring their wings near each other in a mesmerizing display of courtship. I had never seen anything like it before. It was a beautiful reminder of how magical and divine nature is.

Soon it was afternoon, the butterfly artist was long gone, and I hadn't had any visitors in about an hour. Then a group of Hispanic women came into my apartment. One of them was a kind, older woman with gray, wispy hair. Her shirt was a traditional, Aztec style, but it was *purple*, and it had *bunnies* on it.

I couldn't hide the smile that spread across my face. I took that as a sign that my mom really was here, watching over my garage sale with me. I told the lady I liked her shirt, and they got to work, looking around at the various items strewn over the floor, and the multiple garbage bags full of clothes I had gathered.

After some time, the woman came over to me with a bundle of clothes she wanted to purchase. I did the math—I was selling them for three to five dollars apiece—and quoted her $30.

She asked if I could possibly do $20 instead?

So I pulled one of the more expensive shirts out of the pile, and then told her I could do $20 for the rest.

She looked sad. It seemed like that shirt was one of the ones she was most drawn to.

I hesitated, but after a moment I said, "You know what, you can take it."

I decided that this woman would get much more joy and use out of this shirt than I had, and I didn't want to nickel and dime the universe. I would rather make this woman's day.

As I grabbed a bag and started putting her purchases into it, the woman suddenly looked down at her purple bunny shirt.

"Wait, you liked my shirt right?" the woman exclaimed. And then she began to *remove her clothes.*

She took off her cardigan, and pulled the purple shirt up over her head, revealing a white cami underneath. I said nothing while this was happening—to be honest I was a little shocked. I think I may have mumbled out an, "Are you sure?"

But she had already decided. She pulled her cardigan back on and handed me the purple bunny shirt.

I thanked her as she smiled and walked out of my apartment, with the bag of clothes clutched in her hand.

I stood in the center of my apartment and looked down at the shirt in my own hand.

When this woman had walked in, I immediately recognized that shirt as my mom's presence, but I wasn't expecting it to *stay with me.*

How many people do you know, who would take the *literal clothes off their back*, to give to a stranger at a garage sale?

I don't know many. I think this was another encounter with an earth angel.

I had been following my mom's signs for a bit at this point, but this felt like one of the first times I had been given physical, tangible confirmation of her presence. I held the fabric of the shirt against my face and felt closer to my mom than ever.

But more important than the physical shirt itself, was what it represented. This shirt was confirmation that my angels were listening and answering my prayers. Confirmation that I was being divinely guided. Confirmation that I would be backed by their support every step of the way, if I followed the path that they were laying out for me. Confirmation that even though I was embarking on this, at times, very lonely and isolating journey, I was never *actually* alone.

My rabbit heart grew a few sizes that day.

Nowhere to Hide

*I wonder if that fear still creeps up on her
now, though she worked so hard to face
it—I wonder if fears ever really go away,
or if they just lose their power over us.*
—Veronica Roth, *Allegiant*

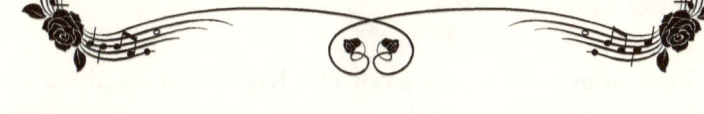

My first Instagram video went viral. I sat in front of the camera and told the story of the bunny garage sale.

I *had* to. I had prayed to my mom, and the next day a woman was taking the *shirt off her back* to give to me? That stuff doesn't just *happen*.

Twelve thousand views.

I stared down at my phone. I should have been happy. This was what I had been *trying* to do when I started posting, when I made my vision board, when I hired Kai.

But I wasn't smiling. I had gotten used to my thirty likes and three supportive comments. I threw my phone onto the couch as if it was hot coal and I was about to be horribly burned.

I lay on my bed, staring up at the ceiling.

Twelve *thousand* people.

Twelve *thousand* people had seen me speak.

Holy fuck.

I put my head in my hands. I kept saying I believed in myself, but I don't think I ever fully did. Because I had not prepared for this.

I had never prepared myself for the possibility that what I was doing would actually *work*.

And now that it had, I was terrified.

It occurred to me how poetic it was, that the one thing I had been most afraid of for my *entire* life was the one thing that I so desperately wanted. The one thing that my soul kept calling me toward, again and again.

To be *seen*.

I rolled over and put my head under my pillow, willing myself to disappear.

I don't know why. I've tried that enough times in my life to know that it won't work.

I got on my next coaching call with Kai. He congratulated me on my viral video, and pulled up my Instagram page to give feedback. He clicked on the bunny video and my voice began playing through my headphones.

I jumped and shook my hands in the air, contorting my face into a knot.

"Ahh, I don't want to hear myself!" I exclaimed in disgust.

"Heather, if you feel that way, you'll never be able to grow," Kai said. "You need to become comfortable witnessing yourself. I want you to close your eyes, lean back in your chair, and pay attention to your thoughts."

I did as he said, and a second later my voice was blaring through my headphones again—social media exposure therapy. I grimaced as if I was in pain. I felt like all I could hear was my whiny, annoying three-year-old voice, floating through the air.

"Let me see! Let me see!"

But this was a twenty-three-year-old's voice. I focused back in, listening to myself speak about holding a garage sale in my apartment.

My brain started to fire attacks at me.

Who are you *to listen to?*

What could you possibly have to say of value?
You sound so annoying.
Why would people give you *any attention?*

Tears formed in my eyes. It was heartbreaking to fully witness the fact that there was still a part of me that hated myself.

I got off my call with Kai and took a deep breath.

I knew that as scared as I was, this was all happening for a reason. I *knew* I needed to be seen. I *knew* I had a message to share. I couldn't do all that if I still doubted my right to take up space.

I had to keep going, as scary as it was. I had to prove to the shadow in my head that I had valuable things to say.

I picked up my phone, hit record on my camera, and began to speak.

HAMMER TIME

I am stronger than the glass. The glass
is as thin as newly frozen ice.
My mind will make it so.
—Veronica Roth, *Divergent*

It was a new day, and I was playing one of my upbeat music playlists as I sifted through more of my belongings. My initial garage sale had barely scratched the surface of everything I needed to purge.

I danced around the apartment, listening to my music and happily throwing things into the center of the room to get rid of. The purple bunny shirt had invigorated me. I was slowly, but surely, building up more confidence to follow the call to leave.

One of my favorite songs began to play. It was "Shatter Me" by Lindsey Stirling, a dubstep violinist. As a violinist myself, I could intensely feel the power and energy of the song. I closed my eyes and listened to the chimes of the intro, spinning and moving my imaginary bow back and forth to the melody.

Soon the tempo began to pick up and the chimes got faster. I paused in the middle of folding an old sweatshirt that I was going to donate. Those chimes sounded awfully familiar …

My eyes widened as I had an epiphany.

This song was about a *music box*.

Mom?

I shrieked and ran over to my phone. Clear as day, the cover art was there—a ballerina holding a violin, trapped inside a cracked music box.

I had seen this cover dozens of times before. *How had I not connected the dots sooner?*

I paid close attention to the lyrics as I continued to gather my things in preparation for my leap of faith, and I couldn't help but shiver at the resonance. I grabbed my phone again and decided to look up the music video.

There Lindsey Stirling stood, in her perfect pink ballerina tutu, playing violin behind the curved glass. Her safe space.

That was me. The rabbit-hearted girl. Frozen in fear.

I was trying to be brave. I was trying to break out. I was trying to break free.

As the video progressed, Lindsey became more and more curious about the gray world on the other side of the glass. She started to play her violin more and more intensely, cracks appearing in the glass as she did. I felt the music swelling up inside of me, urging me to fly higher. As the last chorus began to fade out, the glass finally shattered. Lindsey stood on the grass overlooking a mountain, pieces of broken glass surrounding her feet.

There was an *entire world* waiting for her beyond her little music box.

Wow.

I put my phone down and leaned back in my chair.

What would my life look like if I finally decided to break the glass?

Growing up, my mom's warmth, her presence, the chimes of the music box, that was where I had felt safe. After she left, I had unknowingly created those glass walls around myself. I was living my life trapped in a music box, desperately trying to create some semblance of comfort and security.

I thought that the glass I had created in my mind was keeping me safe, but it wasn't. It was keeping me from living.

Maybe that was why I was so afraid to follow the call. Because part of me knew that if I broke the glass, if I truly started to fly, there would be no going back.

If I take this leap, if I start to fall, there will be no one to catch me.

This would be my first time doing it on my own. No family to back me up—they didn't understand what I was doing. This was a decision I had to make for myself and live out myself. I, alone, would carry the full weight of the consequences of my actions. *And* I was sharing it all on social media. *Everyone* was going to watch me fly, or they were going to see me nosedive. *Was I willing to risk being seen as a failure?*

But I couldn't stop thinking about the words I had written in my journal. The words that weren't mine.

I am guiding you, follow my voice. I have the answers, I have the answers and I want to give them to you, let me.

Maybe no one in the physical world would be around to catch me, but I knew I wasn't taking this journey alone. I knew I had my mom and my angels watching over me. Surely if I followed their guidance, they would hold a net under my newly flapping wings. I could do it if I knew they were with me.

Am I really going to completely blow up my old way of living?

As terrified as I was of change, of the unknown, I also knew that I had hit a breaking point. My life wasn't working as it was. Sure, I didn't know what would happen if I left, but I sure as hell knew what would happen if I stayed. The same misery, the same discontentment, the same discomfort of knowing that I was meant to be somewhere else, but being too terrified to take a step. I couldn't do that anymore. I could not let my life descend into *Groundhog's Day*.

At the end of my life, I don't think I would ever look back and regret trying to fly. I think I would regret never finding out if the air can flow beneath my wings.

What if all of us have the capability to fly, and we live our whole life never knowing, never reaching our full potential, because we don't have the courage to break the glass?

That could not be me. I *could not* let that be me. That is my version of hell.

I put the "Shatter Me" song on repeat to build up my confidence. For hours and days on end. Anytime doubt about jumping on that plane started to creep back in, I would speak the bridge of that song over and over to myself like a mantra.

As scared as I was, there was nowhere to go but forward. I had to know. I had to know what was on the other side of the glass. I had to know what it was like to try to fly.

Someone get me a hammer.

DÉJÀ VU

Now *here,* you see, it takes all the running
you can do, to keep in the same place.
—Lewis Carroll, *Through the Looking-Glass
and What Alice Found There*

Anticipation was in the air on a cloudy Sunday morning as Morgan and I packed our bags into my red Mazda CX-3. We were going to drive up to Sequoia National Park for the weekend.

It was something Morgan had wanted to do for a while. Then one day, she realized that time kept passing her by, and the things she *intended* to do always got pushed further and further away. Everything she wanted to do was always *someday*, not *now*. So a few months back, she marked Sequoia National Park down on her calendar for the first weekend in October to make sure it would happen. As the date got closer and closer, we became friends, so it turned into a girls' trip. I was excited to share an experience with her that she had been looking forward to for so long. I was also excited to see giant trees that were thousands of years old.

We got in the car and I put a nearby cafe into the map so we could grab breakfast on the way to the park. The place was called Swami's in La Mesa, California. When we arrived, we could see the town was clearly preparing for a big event. Dozens of vendor tents covered the asphalt. My gaze landed near the center of the square, where a giant inflatable foaming beer mug sat next to a large banner:

La Mesa Oktoberfest.

I gasped. I had *been there before.* It was one of my earliest photojournalism assignments a year ago, back when I was fresh out of college and still looked at the broadcast news world with fascination and wonder.

I stared at the giant foaming beer, remembering the tilt shot I used to capture it 365 days ago. I walked past the entrance to the beer garden and could see myself standing next to my tripod, with my camera—the one people always commented was too big for a small girl like me—filming all the festival goers.

Hair pulled back into a low pony bun. Black graphic tee with some distorted yellow smiley faces on it. Red cargo shorts and a wide black belt. Beat-up, high-top white Air Forces. Pierced nose and dangling silver chain earrings.

Back then, I dressed as if I had something to prove.

Maybe that was how I burned out so fast. I spent so much mental energy trying to make myself belong in a place that I didn't.

The story of my life. I realized that that was why it was so hard to figure out who I was when I stripped everything away. Because I have always been a shapeshifter, molding myself to other people's perceptions.

What is left of a chameleon when you take away all its colors?

I stared at the exact patch of asphalt where my tripod legs once stood until my vision got fuzzy. It felt both like yesterday and a lifetime ago. It was a bit of a mind fuck.

I've started to coin these moments as Post Spiritual Awakening Flashbacks (PSAF).

PSAF are those déjà vu moments, moments that I've lived before, except when I lived them the first time, I was asleep. Now I am awake to a whole new level of reality, and so the memories I have feel foreign to me. I lived one life, and now I am in another.

It's a jarring experience.

I looked up once again at the giant inflatable mug of beer. I couldn't help but feel a little bit of doubt start to creep back in. A year ago, maybe I felt out of place, but at least I knew what my path looked like and what my identity was.

I was a photojournalist.

Now, all my dreams were in my head. And I was making decisions based on angels. People would think I was off my rocker.

They already did.

I knew I was supposed to have faith, but it was scary. Leaping into the unknown was terrifying. But despite all this, I could see my visions *so clearly* in my mind's eye. There was no way that all this could be a coincidence.

I took a deep breath.

It didn't *have* to make sense to anyone else. It was *my* life. I was the one holding the pen. And soon, all the ideas swirling around through my head would be onto paper, as my new life's story.

Until then, I would let people call me crazy. They always call trailblazers crazy, before the whole world realizes they were the sane ones.

How did I get to this point?

The world around me was exactly the same, but it all looked so different.

I was the one who had changed.

WONDERLAND

> At least I know who I *was* when I got up
> this morning, but I think I must have been
> changed several times since then.
> —Lewis Carroll, *Alice's Adventures
> in Wonderland*

I reserved a tent right off the entrance to Sequoia National Park. Morgan and I walked up to the campsite, bags in hand. A sign off to the left said *Sequoia Jewel*.

Beyond it was a small dirt clearing with a fire pit, and to its left, a picnic table with some kitchen supplies, encased by a clear canopy. In the back of the clearing was a large tent, around fifteen feet tall at its peak, situated on top of a wooden platform. Inside was a table and two full beds.

Real beds in a tent—not traditional camping, but as close to it as I had been in at least a decade.

It was evening when we arrived. We planned to wake up early to enter the park the next morning. The night was ours.

As we started opening our bags, Morgan pulled out a few white plastic Ziplocs.

Mushrooms.

Her friend had given them to her when he heard about our trip.

"No pressure," Morgan said, "But my friend gave these to me, if you're interested in trying them."

Mushrooms?

I had never had any. The only recreational drug I had consumed in the past was weed.

The anxious girl I was six months ago—the one who was pre-scribed Xanax just to get on a plane—would not have dared to say the next words out of my mouth. But lately, I'd decided that I would try almost anything once. We only have one life to live, after all. I wanted to make sure that I'd actually lived mine.

"Fuck it."

I grabbed one of the white bags. It said 1.0g on the side in black Sharpie. I ripped it open, tilted the bag toward my lips, and let the crushed mushroom flakes fall into my mouth.

I immediately grimaced and chugged some water. It tasted like fish food.

Morgan took her own fish dinner, and then we sat around the pit and made a fire. By this point, it was pitch black outside. And we were in the middle of the woods.

But I wasn't scared. I knew my angels had a hand over me.

For triple protection though, I did grab a lighter and my sage—I had brought it with me up to Sequoia, to clear our tent of negative energy. I ignited the flame of my lighter and let it sit under the faded green sage leaves.

After a few moments, I blew out the flame and the sage smoke began to waft into the atmosphere. I held out the leaves as I walked around our fire pit, creating a protective circle around the space.

I started laughing. I felt like SpongeBob when he drew an anti-sea-bear circle in the sand. In that episode, only a perfect circle could protect them from the vicious sea bear.

My sage circle would do the same for us. But with land bears.

After sealing the space, I sat down in one of the deck chairs. Morgan and I put on music, stared at the fire, and began talking.

About life. About everything. The type of conversations that you leave, not necessarily remembering the exact content of what was said, but knowing that the feelings it leaves you with have had a profound impact on you.

We continued talking as I stared deeper into the fire. The longer I stared at the flames, the more the flames became more than just flames. Looking down into the embers, I could see faces, even whole cities, sitting there beneath the glow of the firewood. It felt like I was looking at a lost civilization. At Atlantis. The fire was living, breathing. There was life there.

Morgan saw it too. We spent a while talking about the different forms the embers were creating and deconstructing before our eyes.

I decided to play a song I felt would fit this moment. I opened my phone and typed *I Love You by RIOPY* into the search bar. My favorite piano song.

Light and airy notes began to drift through the air, like a fairy flying through the sky. An already magical moment turned to pure fantasy—I've always loved how music can make any normal experience feel divine.

I raised my hands toward the fire and fluttered my fingers along with the notes.

I was conducting the music of the fire people.

They liked my work. They danced even more vibrantly. It felt as if I was pulling energy from the music and putting it into the fire, as the fire people sent their energy back to me.

As the song continued, the usual orange and blue tinges of flame began to turn purple. Morgan and I watched in awe as the purple flames wisped into the air, and I continued to conduct their movement with my hands.

I thought to myself, *This moment is pure magic.*

So then I did what we have been programmed to do when we want to remember something. I took out my phone and tried to take a picture.

Surely this is the way to immortalize my experience, I always think to myself.

But it wasn't the same. My phone doesn't perceive things the same way I do. It doesn't understand. My phone flattens things.

There are so many images sitting in my phone right now. Memories, I call them. But they aren't. Not really. I stare at the pictures and realize I can remember what happened, but I can't relive it. Because, in fact, I never really lived it the first time. How sad it is to look back on so many experiences in my life that I was just cataloging and documenting, cataloging and documenting—uploading half-baked memories to my iCloud.

My iPhone storage was full, but my soul was empty.

A picture might be worth a thousand words, but a truly lived experience in the present *is an entire novel.*

So I turned off my phone and went back to the fire. I stared and stared, determined to soak up every last drop of this moment.

I pinched myself. *I want to remember this.*

Slowly, but surely, the fire began to die out. The purple dancers began wisping into nothingness. The flames got smaller, and the embers gave one final glow—one last sigh of breath—before fading to black.

I stared at the pit of ashes. My face fell, and for a few seconds I was sad that such an enchanting experience was over.

But then I stopped myself, because I realized something.

The fire *needed* to end.

Endings are necessary. If the fire never died out, I would stop taking the time to appreciate and honor its flames. But now that it had, the memory will live on in my mind.

The same is true of everything else we value in life. *If you grasp hold of something so tightly because you're afraid it will end, the physical situation might not end, but its meaning and the feeling it first gave you, will.*

We are all so scared of endings, and we try to avoid them at all costs. That used to be me, but not anymore.

I've always held on so tightly. It's time to let go and live.

Directionless

1. It is not your fault.
2. It is your responsibility.
3. It is unfair that this is your thing.
4. This is your thing.
5. This will never stop being your thing until you face it.
—Laura McKowen, *We Are the Luckiest*

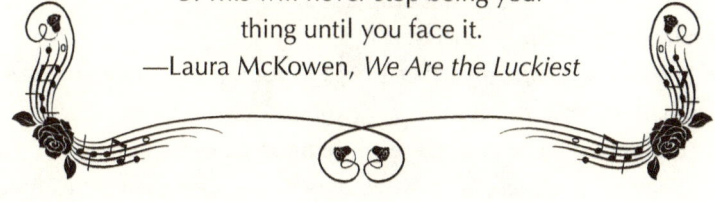

I've always had very big emotions. No one understood them, least of all me.

There's a moment that has always stuck out to me. It was August of 2018, and I was sitting with my family in a hospital room in North Carolina.

It all happened so quickly. One moment we were sitting on the porch of our beach rental, watching the ocean waves, and the next, Mom was shivering, and I was running to grab her water.

The doctors said it was an infection from the heart surgery she had undergone in May. The one that had gone so well that she was supposed to have another twenty years, at least.

We had driven down to North Carolina in two cars, so now we were talking logistics of returning home to New York. My sisters and I would drive back up with one car. My mom and dad would stay in North Carolina until Mom was stable enough to travel, and then they would make the drive back to join us. We lived in Hudson

Valley, New York, but my sisters lived in New York City. So when we returned, I would be in charge of driving them to the train station.

Drive them to the train station?

My phone had broken, so I didn't have maps. *What if I get lost driving home from the train station, and I have no phone to call for help, and I am driving back to an empty house?*

My fear felt huge. I began to freak out, my mind catastrophizing. The "what ifs" swirling in my head threatened to take control and drown me.

Everyone snapped at me for bringing up my concerns. "Heather, why is that what you're thinking about right now? Mom is in the hospital, have some perspective!"

I got so overwhelmed that I began sobbing and ran to the hospital bathroom in the corner of the room. I stayed in there for a few minutes, huddled on top of the white tile, face wet with tears.

I felt so ashamed, so mad at myself. Because they were right. Mom *was* in the hospital. It wasn't about me. And yet, I couldn't stop crying. I couldn't stop the emotions from coming.

Eventually, I heard the outside get quiet. I slowly pulled on the door handle and went back out into the room. Mom was sitting in a chair in the corner, dressed in a white hospital gown. She told me that everyone had gone to the car and would wait for me there while I calmed down.

I started crying harder, and Mom began to console me—always a mom, always strong for her kids, even at a time when her own strength was waning.

I can no longer remember exactly what Mom said to me in that moment, but what I do remember is that she *understood*. She understood why I was so upset. She understood me in ways I hadn't even yet begun to fully understand myself.

She saw beneath the surface. She knew that it wasn't actually about maps and directions and train stations. Below that, deep in my subconscious, was something much darker—something so terrible that I wasn't able to name or say it out loud.

It was the terror of the fact that my mom might *not* be invincible. That the anchor I had grown up with, was herself vulnerable to the ocean.

If Mom is my rock, and she starts to crumble, what will be left of me?

Everything about life as I knew it would start crashing down around me.

My mind could not even fathom what that would look like. That's why I had relentless optimism to the point of denial—through the infection, through the stroke, through the brain surgery, through the coma, up until the hour she died.

And that's why in the hospital that day, I started freaking out about train station directions.

I didn't want to drive my sisters to the train station. Because Mom was supposed to do that. And if I was doing it, that meant Mom wasn't okay.

I needed her to be okay.

Back in my little San Diego apartment, I got on a phone call with one of my sisters. My voice wobbled with hesitation—we had not talked since I had left my news job. I told her about my passion for the spiritual work I was trying to get into, and the success I'd had so far in building my social media presence and business.

She responded to say that she would always love and support me, but she didn't really understand what I was doing at all.

A heaviness began to settle into my chest. I was drifting farther away from her. I was becoming too *different*.

I knew where she was coming from. I did. Because I wouldn't

have understood what I was doing either, up until three months ago, when I was called.

That didn't make it any less difficult to process.

What came out of my mouth next shocked me though.

"I totally understand that, but it won't deter me from what I'm doing, because I know where I'm going. I love you too. I hope you can respect me and trust me enough to know that I can make my own decisions."

That was a big step for me, to stand strong in myself, even when it didn't align with my own family. As an adult, I had gotten into the habit of diluting myself in any and all relationships—to be digestible, to be understood, to be loved. But in that moment, I finally got to a place where I was confident enough in myself that I was willing to stand alone.

As proud of myself as I was, I got off that phone call and cried for at least an hour.

It was heartbreaking, realizing that in finding myself, in starting to lay the building bricks for who I wanted to become, I was also building a wall between me and the people I loved.

I grabbed my phone and opened Instagram to curb the loneliness. The new 10k follower stamp graced the top of my profile.

@awakeningheather.

Ten. Thousand. Followers.

How did everything change so fast?

I scrolled through my comments and DMs—people thanking me for inspiring them, for guiding them, for giving them a direction.

I turned off my phone and put my head in my hands, my body racking with sobs.

Where am I going?

After a moment, I lifted my head and glanced around at my apartment. Through vision stained with tears, I looked at my growing altar, at everything I was preparing to leave behind—as the pile got bigger and bigger, so did the aching hole inside my chest.

I guess if you want to break free, first you have to *break*.

I took a deep breath, picked myself up off the floor, and went back to sorting through the clothes in my closet. As terrified as I was, I knew why I was doing this. I knew there were people I was meant to help.

ALEX WITH THE HELPING HAND

Books can do many things, but not
everything. We have to live the important
things, not read them. I have to …
experience my book.
—Nina George, *The Little Paris Bookshop*

Alex with the Hat was on his way over to help me with the landmine that was slowly becoming my apartment.

We'd kept in contact, and both of our *fuck-it* life decisions were evolving rapidly. He had quickly realized that his time in San Diego wasn't meant to be short-lived, so he had flown back to New York to go through his possessions, and then drove his car across the country back to Ocean Beach, where he had found an apartment to rent.

I, on the other hand, had realized that I was supposed to leave Ocean Beach. And I had a *lot* of stuff to sift through and get rid of before I could. It was really hard to be able to think clearly and find the motivation alone. *Where do I start?*

So Alex was coming to help me get more organized. I was so grateful, and, at the same time, it was very difficult to accept anyone helping me. I had learned that I can't depend on anyone but myself.

Now I was beginning to learn a different lesson. Sometimes, even if we think we can do everything alone, it's better to ask for help. Sometimes, we need others to reignite the flame of faith within us, when our own is waning.

Alex arrived—sans hat—and we began organizing and sorting things into piles. The longer he was there, the more I felt my over-whelm dissipating. It was so helpful to have someone to bounce ideas off of. I realized just how much time in the past month I had spent simply stuck in my own mind.

As much as he helped, his questions also tested my conviction in my plan.

"Are you really going to get rid of all this?" he asked. "I mean, this is a lot of stuff. You don't want it anymore?"

Some of it I didn't need. Other things were hard to part with. And yet, I knew if I was truly serious about traveling, I couldn't hold on so tightly. Anything I kept would all just collect dust anyway—it all needed to go.

"I've spent my whole life collecting things, Alex," I began.

It was true. Sometimes from one obsession to another, but the collector's tendencies always remained. Music boxes, elephant stat-ues, things I deemed as "memories" from my childhood, books, Squishmallows, mini things … The material world was my vice, and it came in all shapes and sizes over the years.

But then I sat surrounded by my possessions, realizing the one thing I didn't own was the one thing I truly wanted, and it couldn't be bought at the store.

A life.

"I no longer want to be a collector of *things*. I want to be a collector of *experiences*."

He nodded and turned back to the kitchen cupboard he was sifting through.

His doubt made me all the surer of myself, and I defiantly grabbed a whole pile of clothes I had been struggling to let go of and added them to the altar.

I set aside one box for keepsakes, one for books, and one suitcase of warm clothes—I knew I would be back in the States for Christmas.

The rest had to go.

Only one box for books? How painful that was. There were so many I still had to get rid of.

But maybe there are some things in life I can't experience through the pages of a book.

Thailand.

An absolutely terrifying idea. It seemed like a pipe dream. Sure, I was becoming more confident, but we were talking *holding my head up high on a walk* kind of confident. Go to Southeast Asia by *myself?* That would *never* happen.

And yet, I couldn't get the idea out of my head. I started instinctively turning the driver's wheel any time I drove by a Thai restaurant, hoping that I could one day buy enough Thai iced teas to wash away the fear flowing through my veins.

So the next day when Alex suggested we go for food, I proposed Thai food. A bell rang as we walked through the door of Social Thai Kitchen in Ocean Beach.

I ordered my usual—a Thai iced tea and pad Thai—and Alex ordered soup.

Soon enough, the waitress brought out our order, and I began stuffing my face with the glassy noodles, trying—and failing—to twirl them around on my fork like you're supposed to. I'd easily had a dozen pad Thais in the past month or so, but I still hadn't come any closer to learning proper table etiquette.

Alex brought a spoonful of soup up to his lips and blew, "I can't believe I just got here and now you're leaving," he said, and popped the now-cool soup into his mouth.

I nodded, a twinge of melancholy aching in my chest. It felt like a cruel twist of fate that I'd been in San Diego for over a year, struggling to make friends outside of work, and now the most aligned authentic people were being brought into my life—right as I was about to move on.

"You'll just have to come meet me in Thailand I guess," I said, grinning in between sips of my tea.

Even as I said it, I doubted if *I* would ever make it to Thailand, let alone *him*.

"Yeah, I guess so," he replied with a smile.

I continued eating my noodles, letting myself get lost in the fantasy of a Heather jetting off to places unknown and traveling the world without fear—touching down in Southeast Asia simply because she wanted to go, and she had decided a long time ago that she was done waiting around for people to be ready to join her.

A nice fantasy. It didn't sound at all like me though.

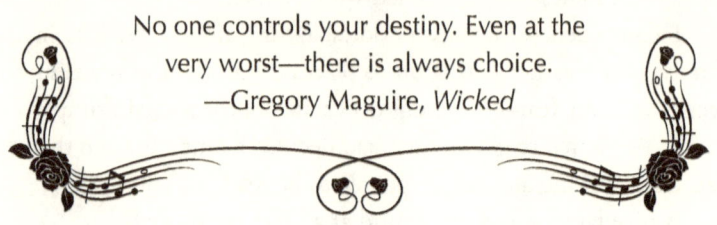

44

THE LAND OF OZ

No one controls your destiny. Even at the
very worst—there is always choice.
—Gregory Maguire, *Wicked*

I spent the morning sorting through more of my belongings, and then inspiration hit me and I decided. Today would be the day I would buy a backpack. If I invested money in my new nomadic life, that would make it harder to turn back.

I walked over to my pile of stuff to purge, and grabbed the black cushioned box sitting on the top. Inside was an emerald necklace. I had won it when I appeared on *Let's Make a Deal* back in August.

Back when I wasn't sure if I believed in angels. Back when being on TV, playing and acting excited for exorbitant prizes, was fulfilling a dream of mine.

Now I had different dreams.

I had planned to pawn the necklace before I moved out. So I grabbed the jewelry box and my wallet and headed out the door. I would buy a backpack, and then head to the pawn shop.

I drove up to REI—an outdoor recreation store—and walked through the glass doors. I entered a giant room full of backpacks, water bottles, hiking boots, and more.

My breath caught in my throat—it was a bit overwhelming. In that moment, I realized the potential insanity of what I was doing. I had never been an outdoorsy person. I had never even set foot in an REI. Now I was going to fly abroad and live nomadically in three weeks.

But I wasn't going to let the fear and doubt stop me. I walked toward the back of the store where a slew of backpacks lined the walls. I had come in with the intention of walking out with a backpack the same day, but I was also hoping that they would have the color I had been envisioning for myself, a deep green color.

As I made my way to the towering backpack wall, I saw it. My backpack. It was the exact color I had imagined. I spoke to the salesperson, and they helped fit me with the correct size. He even put two ten-pound weights into the pack so I could get a feel for walking around with it.

I spent five minutes walking around the store, strapped into this new life of mine. The backpack felt awkward—it straightened my back in a way I wasn't used to. It felt like a new shoe I hadn't yet worn in.

But I still knew. This was *my* backpack. In time, it would cling to my back like a second skin.

There were just a few old layers of self I needed to shed first.

I made the purchase and walked out across the parking lot. I opened the door of my Mazda, threw the pack onto the passenger's seat, and got into the car. After buckling my seatbelt, I turned to look over at the seat. The backpack I had just purchased sat on the left, and the necklace I intended to pawn sat on the right.

Something on the tag of the backpack caught my eye. I picked it up and leaned in to get a better look. Underneath the item description and the barcode, was one word.

Emerald.

I gasped and opened the jewelry box to reveal the bright green stone I had been planning to sell later that day.

Emerald.

I sat dumbfounded for several minutes, glancing between the

backpack and the necklace.

Between my *two emeralds*.

This is the moment, I thought to myself. The time where I would finally decide for *myself* what *I* actually value.

I thought back to my conversation with Alex. "I no longer want to be a collector of *things*. I want to be a collector of *experiences*."

For so long I had lived with a consumeristic cloud over my eyes, but now I saw everything so clearly. I would happily give up comfort, stability, luxury, and money, for my time, for memories, and for the expansion that comes from pursuing new experiences and interacting with new people.

If that makes me crazy according to the world we live in, then I don't want to be sane. I want to *live*. To me, true insanity is working away to make more money, to buy more items that simply represent your status in the world. We have been *programmed* to want them. They don't actually mean *anything*. It's all an *illusion*.

Despite my fears, staring down at those two emeralds made it abundantly clear what I had to do. I must move forward. I must see what's on the other side of this door. Because I knew what lay behind. Necklaces and parties and the perfect throw pillows to go with your sofa and the cute picket fence standing in front of your too-green lawn. Apartments with high ceilings and chandeliers and glasses of wine …

That is someone else's dream.

I put the car into drive and pulled out of the parking lot with a new resolve. I had chosen my emerald. I needed to see it through.

This was the beginning. I was starting a new life. And it would begin in three weeks, as I sat on a plane, flying toward jungles far away.

LAURA'S DREAM

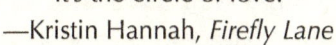

You were struggling to break free of being
my daughter but unsure of how to be
yourself, while I was afraid to let you go.
It's the circle of love.
—Kristin Hannah, *Firefly Lane*

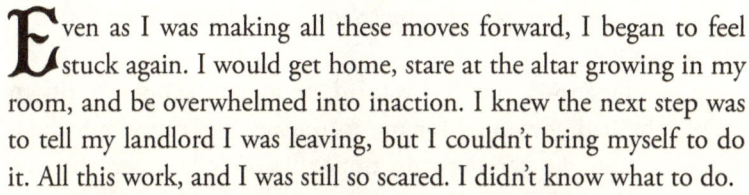

Even as I was making all these moves forward, I began to feel
stuck again. I would get home, stare at the altar growing in my
room, and be overwhelmed into inaction. I knew the next step was
to tell my landlord I was leaving, but I couldn't bring myself to do
it. All this work, and I was still so scared. I didn't know what to do.

I got on another coaching call with Kai, feeling dejected.

One thing you should know about Kai is that he is a psychic. He
can read you like a book. There's not much you can hide from him.

You don't have to believe me. I used to not believe in psychics.
But then I met Kai. And he told me things about myself he shouldn't
have been able to see. And then I began meditating every day, and
my own psychic abilities started to come online.

I told him about how I was feeling blocked and in my head that
week. As I spoke, he suddenly put his hands together in prayer and
closed his eyes.

I laughed. I knew enough by now to know this meant he was
about to channel a higher power, and then tell me some super accu-
rate and personal information about myself that he had no way of

knowing, and that I wouldn't want to hear, but that I needed to hear. I waited to see what it was.

I wasn't expecting what he said next.

"You need to let go of your mom a little bit," Kai began. "You're holding on too tightly to her. She's here with you, because she knows you need her. But you're keeping her from moving on. What's something that you want, that's against what she would've wanted for you?"

I leaned back in my chair like a balloon deflated.

Let go of my mom?

I thought *reconnecting* with my mom was what had brought along this whole healing journey in the first place. I thought that *she* was the one guiding me. *She* was the one who had led me to Kai. I was following the music. I was living life in her image.

Now I had to take a step back?

Not only that, but I had a hard time answering his question.

What's something that I want, that's against what Mom would've wanted for me?

I had no answer. She had wanted me to get the opportunity to travel. She had advocated for me to pursue my creativity in high school, despite the starving artist trope that pushes so many parents to stifle their kids' dreams. She *always* wanted what I did. She *always* wanted me to follow my dreams. She never cared what it looked like. She just wanted me to be *happy*.

I left the call with Kai's words echoing around in my mind.

What's something that I want, that's against what my mom would've wanted for me?

A few days passed and the question still burned in the back of my mind.

Then, one day, I found myself thinking about Mom. About the music box in my apartment. And about her tombstone.

My mom's death had been very unexpected. My family didn't know how to handle it. I blinked and it was ten months later. I was visiting her grave, still without a tombstone.

The only marker of Mom's presence was a small, green framed name placard that they put there the day she was interred. It spelled her last name wrong.

I stared at the misspelling and got choked up. Mom deserved better.

So I went home and began the process of designing her tombstone. I reached out to the company the cemetery suggested and scrolled through their website for the different carving options they had. I remember how excited I had been when I came across an option that had a lighthouse carved across the top.

If you remember anything about my mom, let it be that she was a beach girl. We went to the same secluded island off North Carolina for vacation every year. We went shelling in the mornings, and we sat by baby sea turtle nests at night to see if they would hatch. We visited the local lighthouse, and we sat on the porch listening to the crashing of the ocean waves. She loved to fall asleep to the sound of the waves. Her plan had always been to retire and move to that small island.

So I had proposed the lighthouse design. I wanted to bring a bit of that island to her. I even got the company to add a small carving of a sea turtle near the bottom. My sisters agreed it was a perfect representation of Mom and the resting place she would have wanted.

Then we had to decide on a quote.

There was a quote she had loved. A quote that she had on a mug while we were all growing up. It was one of her favorite mugs—one of us accidentally broke it when we were younger, and we knew it made her sad.

This quote was even written by a Nancy Thayer—the same name as her mother, my nana. The quote was, "My heart will always be in a cottage by the sea."

It just felt right. Her body could rest there in the ground, but her heart, her soul, was in a seaside cottage listening to the waves. Where she was always meant to be.

That phrase had slowly drifted back to me over the past few months—when I saw the music box, when I spoke my mom's name, when I began to see signs of her in the world all around me. It had all started when I moved into that apartment …

My heart will always be in a cottage by the sea.

Mom was in that apartment. I knew it. I felt her there.

My heart ached as it dawned on me, what Kai had been trying to get at—but he had been asking the wrong question.

The question wasn't, *What's something that I want, that's against what my mom would've wanted for me?*

It was the opposite.

It was, *What's something my mom wanted, that's against what I want for myself?*

When I first moved in, I had called this place my dream apartment. And I had thought it was. Cute, vintage charm, right by the ocean … It seemed like a cottage. It reminded me of my old home back in New York.

But then I realized that it wasn't *my* dream. It felt like someone else's. And in this moment, I finally realized whose it was.

It was *my mom's* dream.

This wasn't my apartment. This was *Mom's* apartment.

I think a deep-rooted part of me felt guilty that her life was cut short. That she wasn't able to retire and go live in a cottage by the beach like she had always planned. So I unknowingly began living out her dream for her. I was carrying out a subconscious mission to finish her life, rather than go and live my own.

This apartment was Mom's dream. My dream was to fly. To travel. To explore.

I had to let go. I had to take the leap.

That day I realized, no matter the fear, I had to get out. The life I was living was not mine. My mom would want me to follow my *own* path.

The day I get on that flight, that is the day I start living my life for me.

BREAK THE CIRCLE

To find growth is to communicate … And
whether you get the response you deserve,
that is not so much the point. The point is
having the courage to say, "I know my own
heart, what it wants, needs, and deserves."
—Courtney Peppernell, *Time Will Tell*

I'd been preparing to move abroad like my angels were telling me to—but I still hadn't told my landlord I was leaving.

I knew it was what I had to do, but I was terrified. Giving up the apartment finally made it *real*.

Because even as I did all the preparation, there was still room to walk back to safety. I could easily decide to stay, and just have a new backpack in my possession and live in a much emptier apartment. There was still room for me to turn around. The safety net was there.

We talk so much about what we want in our wildest dreams, all these endless possibilities, but actually trying to take steps toward them in the real world? That is a *whole* different ballgame.

Ending my lease meant throwing away my safety net. It meant regardless of what I did or where I decided to go, I would be without a homebase on November 1st. No room to turn around.

Not only that, but my landlord was the sweetest man in the world. He had helped me move in my stuff every time I had pulled up with a carload alone. He gave me avocados from his friend's tree and advice about the best street parking. He cared about the wellbeing of the apartment and fixed any issues quickly. He even helped me construct my bed frame. I really valued his help and knowledge at a time when I was moving out on my own for the first time, without another adult to turn to. He said he wanted me to think of him as a neighbor and not a landlord. And he was a nice neighbor. I felt bad telling him I would be leaving.

My face was wet with tears as I turned onto Sunset Cliffs Boulevard. I wiped them away with the back of my hand and fresh ones took their place. I was so *scared*. This was the moment that would finalize everything.

The song changed as I slowed to a stop at the light and glanced up at the dash of my car. *Send Them Off!* the screen said. A song by Bastille.

I laughed. There's my sign. No matter how scared I was, I knew what needed to be done.

I walked back into my apartment, took a deep breath, and collected myself. Then I picked up my phone and texted my landlord.

Hey! Are you home at the moment?

A few minutes later, my phone lit up. A call from my landlord. My heart pounded a bit faster, and I answered the phone.

"Hey, is everything okay? I'm on my way out of town and won't be back until the morning, but if something is wrong in the apartment, I can turn around."

My heart began to ache a little more. Here he was, still being kind and accommodating—more than he needed to be—and here I was, about to end my lease. Even though I thought it might be better to have this conversation in person, I had already worked myself up so much today over making this decision, that I knew it was now or never. So I took a shaky breath and started to come clean.

"Oh, yeah, everything's fine. I actually did have to tell you something though. I had hoped it would be in person, but I guess I can say it over the phone," I began hesitantly. "I'm actually going to be ending my lease and moving out."

My stomach dropped, the way it does right as you start to crest over the hill of a rollercoaster. The anticipation and fear of something coming, without quite knowing exactly what it will be or feel like.

His response made my whole body tense. Not because of what he said, but *how* he said it. I felt his entire demeanor change, even through the phone. The friendly neighbor I had grown accustomed to dealing with was gone.

"I had a feeling this was going to happen when you moved in and said you wanted to travel. I'm not happy at all, I'll tell you that much. When you moved in, we discussed you staying for a year."

This was true; we had. During my apartment tour, he had mentioned that he was hoping for someone who would stay for a longer term. Even so, he had kept the lease on a month-to-month basis. At the time, he said this was because he knew that sometimes life just hits you out of nowhere, and so a month-to-month lease would make it easier for me to leave. Like if I got a job offer in another state, for example.

I had said yes to all this at the time. I was planning to stay for the foreseeable future, but I appreciated that the month-to-month lease gave me flexibility in case a situation *did* arise. Obviously, on that day near the tail end of June, I wasn't anticipating getting initiated by a spirit team I didn't know I had, and being called to quit my fancy adult job, purge everything I owned, and travel to the middle of a jungle in a foreign country.

Sometimes life really *does* hit you out of nowhere.

I couldn't quite tell him all that though. I couldn't tell him that I felt my soul dying the longer I lived in this city, and that I was feeling a deep call to travel. I couldn't tell him that the longer I sat here while that channeled journal message sat on my desk, I withered away more and more. He wouldn't understand the "woo woo" angel explanation. All he had were the logical facts. The ones where I had left my job, and was now deciding to leave my apartment.

"I'm so sorry," I told him. "I just had no way of anticipating that this would happen, and that I would leave my job. And now that I've left it, I can't afford to stay."

That did nothing to appease him. "We had a verbal agreement," he kept repeating. "Now you're going back on your word."

I have to say, this confused me at the time. I really value my commitments and would never intentionally go back on my word. And I didn't think that I was. I knew he had the intention of someone staying for a longer amount of time, but right after that, he explicitly said that he had made the lease on a month-to-month basis for this *exact* reason. For life taking you on unexpected turns. But now that was no longer valid? I started to get overwhelmed and confused.

"Again," I pleaded. "I really didn't mean to do that. I had every intention of staying when I moved in. But things in my life just progressed so fast. You said yourself that you kept the agreement month-to-month because sometimes life comes out of nowhere. That is what happened."

Also the angels are telling me that I need to leave, I thought silently.

How much *easier* it would be to explain my decisions, if everyone saw the world through the same supernatural lens that I did.

I had hoped we could find some common ground by the end of the conversation, but the more I apologized and tried to get him to see my side, the colder and more detached he became. He ended the call by telling me to place an official letter ending the lease in his mailbox.

I ended the call crying.

There's something that they don't tell you about change. It's something I never anticipated, as I sat at the table in Morgan's apartment two months ago, a girl with a head full of dreams and a fist full of magazine clippings, pasting my aspirations onto a corkboard.

It was a truth I was slowly becoming accustomed to as I began to "prepare," like my channeled message had told me to.

And it was a truth that was now hitting me smack in the face.

Change means *loss*.

All those things on your wish list? All the things that you want? The new life you're manifesting? Yeah, well that actually means what it says, *a new life*.

It means *letting go of the old one*.

Maybe it sounds naive of me to say that the Heather who pasted her travel dreams onto that vision board, didn't anticipate needing to give away almost all of her belongings, give up her apartment, say goodbye to comfort, stability, and convenience, leave her job, and say goodbye to her friends. I mean … those would seem like the natural steps to take if I were to start traveling.

But we don't think about all those things when we're living in our fantasy lands—I sure as hell didn't.

That's why it is so much easier to dream, than to see those dreams manifest into reality. Because to start becoming intimate with moving toward your dreams means becoming intimate with death herself.

Death and rebirth. Night and day. Dark and light. One needs to embrace the cycles. To let the wheel of life turn.

On that chilly night in October, my wheel was turning, but not before ripping the cogs and attachments from where it previously sat.

A pile of used tissues steadily grew higher on my desk.

It was so many things at once. It was the overwhelming loneliness and fear of making this decision, even though I knew my family didn't understand me. It was the crushing weight of detaching myself from the emotional bond I had created with this apartment, in the misguided attempt to preserve my mom's memory. It was the grief of knowing that someone I cared about, and had no intention of hurting, now felt slighted.

Sometimes following your path is messy.

I took a deep breath in. This was one of my final tests. I could feel it. To prove if I had really done the work, if I really believed in myself.

Because part of standing strong in your truth and self-concept, means detaching from other people's perspectives of you. Other people's perceptions are out of your control, and they are not your responsibility. I am not perfect, but I am always trying to operate out of my heart space and best intentions. That is what is important.

Not an easy conclusion to come to terms with as a recovering people pleaser. But it was a needed one, especially as I started to put myself out there on social media. Because to do that successfully—to do it without breaking—I needed to learn how to stand tall, and not sway to every misperception or projection thrown my way.

With a renewed sense of clarity, I said a small *thank you* to my angels for continuing to give me the lessons I needed to stand stronger in my power.

I pulled on a sweater and took a walk toward the ocean to clear my head. I stared out at the roaring and foaming of the waves.

Am I really going to do this?

You have to leave.

I felt the cool sand pass through my toes as I walked along the shoreline.

You know you have to leave.

I slowly spun around, looking at the world around me, at the Ocean Beach that had only just become my place to call home three months ago.

You know you have to leave.

I stared at the lights of the main street.

How had time moved so fast? It felt like everyone else was frozen in place, and somehow I was spinning endlessly, dancing across time and space.

Will this whirlwind ever slow down? Will the eye of the storm ever drop me back down to earth, to the people and places that are meant for me? Or am I destined to be forever turning, picking up more speed, a hurricane barreling through towns and civilizations … making waves, but with no shore to call her home?

Time will tell.

47

TAKE THE WHEEL

"She says she wants to see the world," I spoke
through my salty tears. "She's not sure what
her future holds—claims that this is her fate."
—Suzanne Weyn, *Distant Waves*

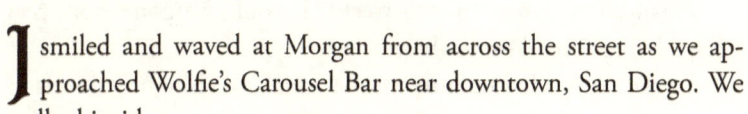

I smiled and waved at Morgan from across the street as we approached Wolfie's Carousel Bar near downtown, San Diego. We walked inside.

"Reservation for Heather," I said.

The waitress grabbed two menus from the stand. Behind her was a giant carousel, glowing with neon yellow lights. She walked us over to the edge, and we slowly stepped onto the rotating platform, taking our seats at the cushioned stools in front of the bar counter.

The carousel moved slowly, slow enough that it felt like you were not moving at all. If you lost track of time, however, you would suddenly look up and be on the other side of the room.

A fitting place to have dinner with "Momo," the girl who taught me the value of losing yourself in a moment in time.

We ordered drinks—mocktails, because at this point, I had decided to go sober—and began catching up. We hadn't spoken in about two weeks, which on *Heather's Spiritual Awakening Timeline*, was about two months.

I picked up my drink and brought it to my lips with shaky hands. I had gone into this night with a bit of hesitation for what I was going to tell Morgan next—I was planning to leave San Diego. To leave the country indefinitely. In two weeks.

I should've told her earlier, but a part of me was so terrified when I channeled that message to leave that I didn't know if I could go through with it. Even as I prepared and started to sell all my stuff, I wondered if I would ever get where I was trying to go. And so I didn't want to tell anyone my plans, in case I couldn't keep my promise to myself. I would have been overcome by shame.

But now the promise I had made to myself was becoming more and more of a reality. So much so that I had to start telling people. And the hardest to tell would be Morgan, who I had grown so close to in such a short amount of time.

I was sad to do it, and a bit terrified. *What would she say?*

Finally, I told her. In two weeks, I would be gone from San Diego, living abroad somewhere.

I wasn't sure what country yet—I wasn't planning my travels in the conventional way. But I knew I would be long gone from this place.

I sat tense, muscles braced, waiting for the reaction.

A smile spread across her face as she raised her head and looked into my eyes.

"Obviously I'm going to miss you, but I'm so excited for you. It feels right. It feels like it makes sense for you to go."

Relief washed over my body and sparked a warmth in my heart that I had not felt in a long time. I suddenly wondered why I was so scared to tell her in the first place.

I realized it was because in the past, I had gotten very used to transactional relationships. In those types of relationships, this news would not go over well. So subconsciously, I braced myself for that reality. The one where the person shoots down my idea and tries to convince me to stay, or gets upset that I didn't care about them enough to want to stay.

But what Morgan and I had was a *real* friendship. And a real friendship means always wanting what's best for the other person. Even if it makes you sad. Even if it means you won't be able to see each other for a long time.

I smiled, with a touch of melancholy that came from knowing this chapter of my life was soon coming to an end.

Just another reminder to be truly present here on this carousel.

We spent the rest of the night debating whether I should go to Costa Rica or Thailand. These were the two countries my intuition—as well as my synchronicities—were pulling me toward.

At the end of the night I hugged her goodbye, got into my car, and couldn't stop myself from smiling the whole drive home.

So this was what unconditional love and support in relationships actually felt like.

It felt good.

BUILD A NEW ONE

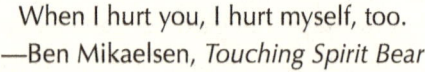

I'm part of some big circle that I don't
understand. And so are you. Life, death, good
and bad, everything is a part of that circle.
When I hurt you, I hurt myself, too.
—Ben Mikaelsen, *Touching Spirit Bear*

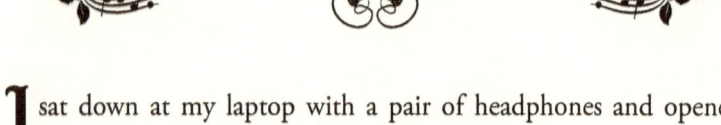

I sat down at my laptop with a pair of headphones and opened Zoom. Jess, the breathwork facilitator from my Temecula retreat, had extended an invite to a virtual breathwork session that afternoon.

I was excited, but I also felt some nerves settling in my stomach. My last breathwork experience—the one where I completely lost control of my hands—was a bit overwhelming. But I also knew it was an important release, and I was about due for another one. As my flight date grew closer, I was getting a bit stuck in my mind.

I turned on my camera and listened as Jess and her husband, Cory, introduced the session. Each session, they said, had a different theme. This month's theme was breathwork for relationships.

I began laughing and looked up at the ceiling. It was a cruel joke my angels were playing.

This was a sore subject for me. At this point, all the relationships in my life were now at arm's length. I wasn't speaking much to my family because they didn't understand what I was doing, and I didn't want them to instill doubt in me about where I was going. I only spoke to my friends every few days or weeks to catch up, and I didn't have too many of them. And I had completely pulled myself out of the dating scene to focus on myself. At that point, one of the only consistent people in my life was my coach, Kai.

That's kind of sad to say. He was only there because I had paid him.

Otherwise, I was alone. And I was cripplingly aware of the fact. Hearing the words "Breathwork for relationships" come out of Jess' mouth felt a bit like a knife to the heart.

But here we were—it was clearly something I needed to work on.

I laid down on my bed and put on my sleeping mask. The music began to play as Cory and Jess coached us through that same three-step breath from the retreat.

Belly, chest, out. Belly, chest, out.

As the music began to build, I felt the tension once again take hold of my body. My hands slowly began to furl into those familiar lobster claws.

But this time, I could handle it. I breathed deeper as I slowly willed myself to unfurl them and gain back control over my limbs.

Kind of like how I was starting to gain back control over my life. Getting back into the driver's seat.

It felt good.

The music got more intense as the time came for us to let out a scream. I pressed my pillow against my face and screamed as hard as I could.

It still wasn't hard enough. There was so much inside of me. I suddenly felt so *angry*. So angry at being misunderstood all my life, at not being treated the way I deserved, at constantly trying to do my best by others and always falling short without fail.

Why was I alone?

I had so much to give. And I had given so much of myself already. I screamed and screamed.

The screaming turned to sobbing. Because as Cory and Jess

talked about feeling love energy, I realized that even after all the work I had done, I was still having a hard time holding love for myself.

How could I really show unconditional love for anyone else if I couldn't show it to myself?

My relationship with myself was reflecting outward. That's why I was alone.

And I would continue to be until I stopped looking at myself like a problem that had to be solved.

As we breathed, I felt my hands start to tingle with love energy. Through Jess' guidance, I tried to pour it back into myself.

I tried to remind myself that I am *just* as deserving of love as anyone else. Even on the days when I make mistakes. On the days when I'm simply *human*. It was so *frustrating* that my brain was not able to see that most of the time.

The music faded away as Cory and Jess ended the session. I rose up from the bed and brought a hand up to my face to wipe away the tears.

We had a discussion about the experience afterwards. Jess asked the group an interesting question, "What are you willing to risk in order to have fulfilling relationships?"

I froze. I immediately knew the answer.

My mind had been living in perpetual fear, that with one wrong move, I would set off another landmine. The only solution was to be perfect. But trying to be perfect had gotten me nowhere.

I opened the chat box, and hesitantly typed out my task:

I need to risk misunderstanding and rejection in order to be loved.

I was so afraid of rejection that I had been repressing my authentic self and holding back my feelings. That fact was the reason why I was alone.

There's a reason why they call it "falling" in love. It is a sacrifice. You must fully sacrifice the ego. Put your heart on the line and know that it is sitting out in the open, primed to be stabbed, but hoping to God that it won't be.

Is this my last sacrifice?

Not leaving behind the stability of my apartment, but the stability that comes from having a closed-off heart.

Maybe becoming the lion-hearted girl isn't about becoming the girl with a heart of armor. Maybe it is about becoming the girl who is strong enough to put her heart out in the open, no matter how many times she's been hurt before, because she knows that true, limitless love equals strength.

Maybe those of us who are the strongest are the ones who are willing to show up as themselves. To fully love and be loved, despite knowing the risks.

Yes, I had been hurt in the past. But in continuing to close myself off, I was just hurting myself more. I had to see what was on the other side of the door. I had to break this cycle of rejection, fear, and self-abandonment.

I had to embody love.

THROUGH THE LOOKING GLASS

"If we look into a broken mirror, a mirror that's
cracked or missing parts, what do we get?"
… "We get a distorted and broken reflection," she said.
"Right," Bailey said. "And if the mirror is whole?"
"We see everything."
—Dave Eggers, *The Circle*

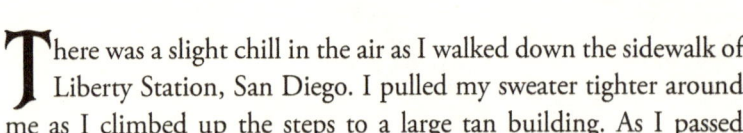

There was a slight chill in the air as I walked down the sidewalk of Liberty Station, San Diego. I pulled my sweater tighter around me as I climbed up the steps to a large tan building. As I passed through the doors, I saw the girl I was meeting and waved her over.

Her name was Sonya. She had long blond hair and a youthful smile. We met a few weeks back at a drum circle during a full moon party—she was another free spirit. So when I saw a post on Instagram for another ecstatic dance, I decided to reach out.

We walked upstairs, removed our shoes, and went through the door into the studio. It was a long space, with windows on one wall and mirrors completely covering the other, giving the illusion that it was even bigger than it was.

This time I knew a little more of what to expect from an ecstatic dance event, so I felt less like a fish out of water as we went through the stretches and exercises. We did a few warrior poses, and as I pulled back my imaginary bow and arrow, I felt myself starting to stand more in my power, rather than acting like the meek little mouse the arrow would be pointing at.

Then the night began and the music lifted me up, as my tight muscles began to melt into softness and fluidity.

I think dancing is when I feel the most myself.

I began to float around the room again. I would fall to the floor, roll my head back, rise up again, feel my body, spin around.

From time to time, a few people even let out animal noises, and a chorus would soon join in. I howled with the pack.

Even though Sonya and I had come together, ecstatic dance is a very individual experience, so we had soon gone our separate ways. But after about an hour or so, I was dancing near the front of the room—facing the center, like I always did. I turned around, and there was Sonya, dancing near the wall.

She wasn't facing the center. She was facing the mirror.

I observed her for a moment. She was doing what I had been doing—dancing in her wildest, most authentic expression—but watching herself as she did.

I stood still and pondered this for a minute. I realized that even as I was building up my confidence, as I was beginning to authentically express myself in front of others, as I was beginning to let people see me as this fluid, sensual person that I wanted to become … was *I* comfortable seeing myself as that? To fully face myself and the woman that I was stepping into?

By facing the middle of the room, I was denying her existence.

In the mirror, there is nowhere to hide.

My mind wandered back to high school. All those school nights, spending hours in front of the mirror, picking the right clothes to wear. All those times spent gazing into the girls' bathroom mirror, making sure my hair and makeup were still intact—in between every class, so much so, it would sometimes make me late.

I was always scrutinizing every fraction of my being to make sure

I was presenting myself well to others. I used to *wish* that there was a floating mirror following me around, so I could always check if I looked presentable without having to run to the bathroom or pull out my phone.

That is an *actual thing* that I wished for as a teenage girl. I lived my *life* in that goddamn mirror.

Over time, the mirror had become a tool of destruction for my self-confidence, magnifying my insecurities and keeping me small.

Maybe it's time that I stand in front of this mirror and reclaim my power.

I walked over to the mirror, a few feet away from Sonya, and locked eyes with myself.

It took me a second to recognize the woman looking back. She was happy. She was confident. She was starting to feel comfortable being herself.

This was not the same me from a few months ago.

But yet, there she was. I was looking right into her green eyes. And there was a beautiful energy about her. A glow. And as I stared into her eyes, I began to smile, because I realized that that woman was me.

I slowly began raising my arms and rolling my hips, doing everything I had the confidence to do when my eyes were closed in the center of the dance floor.

At first, I was worried others would see me dancing with myself in the mirror and think it was vain, but then I realized that I didn't care if people saw it that way.

Because *why shouldn't we?* Why shouldn't we enjoy our time with ourselves? Why shouldn't we be in *love* with ourselves?

You are the only person you will be with forever.

I was going to dance with myself in front of the fucking mirror.

I went a little farther beyond my comfort zone and dropped to the floor again. On my knees with my legs spread open, I continued to dance, roll my head back, and feel my body. It was a bit overwhelming at first, directly confronting my sensuality, when all I had been taught to do was repress it.

Humans are sensual beings. Denying this aspect of ourselves is denying ourselves as a whole. It creates a disconnect, a space between who we are and what we make ourselves appear to be. It leads us to no longer feel safe in our own bodies.

That was how I used to feel, like I had pulled on a skin that was too tight. It was suffocating me. I needed to get out.

But that night, I felt like I could finally breathe. I was present in my own body—for me and no one else. I rose up from the floor, eyes still trained on my own soul. I continued to sway and rock my arms. I felt the music rising as I felt the same power rising within me.

As the music built, I slowly raised both of my arms to the sky, brought my hands together, and lowered them down to my chest. I raised my leg and settled in a tree pose as the beat dropped in the song.

I stayed there, staring intensely into my eyes. I took the energy I felt emanating from the music and poured it back into myself, balanced in total stillness as the world continued to move and flow behind me.

Then, as my gaze deepened, I realized …

I was looking at *her*.

Her—the woman from the garden. The statue, standing tall above the mausoleum.

In that moment, all those chapters ago, I had said that I had met my Higher Self.

But it was a mere glimpse. It was outside of myself, a solid stone representation of what I *could* be.

Now she was *here*. She was *within* me. I *felt* her.

I was staring into her green eyes.

I had walked up to the mirror a few songs ago, apprehensive about its vulnerability, but now I didn't want this time to end.

Because I felt her power. I *felt* it.

It was at this moment that it happened. I came home to myself.

I walked out of that studio and down the sidewalk with a new determination in my soul, and fire in my eyes.

I am the lion-hearted girl.

I have everything I need.

I can do anything.

I Am

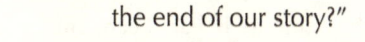

"Do you think, Daniel," she said to him,
rolling over onto her back so that she was
able to look out of the window while she
spoke, "that we might have reached
the end of our story?"
—Maggie O'Farrell, *This Must Be the Place*

It was Halloween night. A year before at this time, I would've been pulling on tights and smearing my face with makeup, on my way to a party where I'd drink until I could no longer see my reflection in the murky brown liquid of a red solo cup.

But this year, I didn't care to play dress up. I had spent my entire life wearing masks. I just wanted to be *me*. So I stayed home.

This was no ordinary night, not because there were small children wearing white sheets and skipping with candy as I walked down the sidewalk, but because it was my last night in Ocean Beach. The next day I would be officially moving out of my apartment, and the morning after that, I would be getting on a one-way flight out of the country.

I walked toward the shore and laid my towel out on the sand. I stared at the ocean waves for a long time. After a while, I turned and glanced back toward the city.

I saw the parking lot, the one where only four months earlier, I had been sitting with a boy who lived out of a van, hanging onto his

235

every word because I didn't know that all the love and validation I needed was inside of me.

I glanced at the rocky path, the one where I sang "Dream A Little Dream of Me" until my anxiety melted away, where I learned that I could reclaim my peace without the help of anyone else.

I looked at the street corner, the one where I learned to dance like no one was watching.

My gaze moved toward the pier, the one where I learned to fish, and more importantly, to be patient as you cast your line in life's ocean.

Everything was the same as it had been, but it all seemed so different now. I found myself perplexed about how one little beach town could spark such a fast and profound inner transformation within me.

There was something magical about Ocean Beach. I felt it the first time I came here.

Now I have captured that magic, and it lives within me.

It felt like my San Diego life needed a proper goodbye. So I pulled out my journal—I had traded my childhood black and white marble cover for a yellow one—put pen to paper, and began to write:

Goodbye San Diego.

Part of me will miss you, but it's not enough to stay. We've outgrown each other, and now I need to move on. I've always held on too tightly after things have lost their luster.

Words cannot describe how grateful I am for our time together. You will always be the city where I was reborn. Where my life began again.

You were a catalyst. A stepping stone. But your purpose has been filled. There's nothing left for me here.

I am ready now. The planes pass overhead, and I feel the rumbling in my bones. I know I am meant to be in the air and not on this ground.

So tonight, I will shed a tear for the times that we had together, but tomorrow I will move forward and not look back. This is where our story ends. I am long overdue for a new chapter. For a whole new book.

I've been grasping too tightly. My hands are unfurling. I'm letting you go now. May you be a safe haven for more wandering souls, kindred spirits, and wild women such as myself.

I'll never forget our time together. It was here that I was Becoming.

But now, I Am.

I. Am. Moving. On.

-heather ♥

"Have we reached the end?" asked Piglet.
"Yes," I replied. "I suppose so."
"It *seems* to be the end," said Pooh.
"It does. And yet—"
"Yes, Piglet?"
"For me, it also seems like a beginning."
—Benjamin Hoff, *The Te of Piglet*

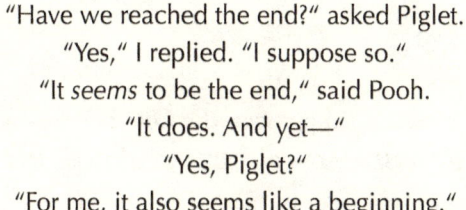

I'd Love to Hear from You!

Thank you so much for taking the time to read *Break Free*. Your feedback is incredibly valuable and helps other readers discover my story.

If you enjoyed this book, I would greatly appreciate it if you could take a few moments to leave a review. Whether it's a few words or a detailed account, your thoughts and experiences can make a big difference, and it would mean the world to me to be able to read them.

—heather ♥

To leave a review, simply **scan the QR code below** or visit
www.athenarosealchemy.com/break-free

WELCOME TO
MY WORLD ♥

Words cannot describe how much it means to me that you've made it to the end of my story. Completing *Break Free* is a big milestone, but it's only the beginning. I'd love to stay connected and continue offering support on your journey. Here are the best ways we can continue to grow together:

Connect with Me on Instagram
A lot has happened since I first hopped on that plane all those months ago! I have recently made the shift from @awakeningheather to @athenarosealchemy on Instagram to reflect the integration of everything I have learned on my spiritual journey thus far. Stay connected with me by following @athenarosealchemy, where I continue to share insights from my personal journey, along with tips and guidance to support you on yours.

Join My Podcast
In my podcast, *Paradoxical*, I explore any and all topics about life, my healing journey, my take on spirituality, my travels, neurodivergence … *Nothing* is off limits. Learn more about my podcast and how to tune in on the next page!

Explore More Resources on My Website
Go to **www.athenarosealchemy.com/break-free-bonuses** for free access to the *Break Free Scrapbook*, a meditation guide, reflection questions, and other additional resources! On my website you'll also discover pathways for more individualized support, and the most up-to-date information on ways we can work together.

THE PARADOXICAL PODCAST

Par·a·dox·i·cal
/ˌperəˈdäksək(ə)l/
adjective
Seemingly absurd or self-contradictory; goes against common sense or expectations; containing two opposing ideas in a way that seems impossible or difficult to understand, but may contain a hidden truth

Ex: The more I learn about the world, the more I realize just how little I know anything.

I've spent so much of my life focusing on labels, trying to define myself, to make myself more easily consumable to the masses. But I've realized that labels don't work on me. They stick and get peeled off just as quickly.

It's ironic, because I'm someone who loves words. I'm an author now for God's sake. And yet my throat closes off when I'm asked to describe myself to someone new. I've written and rewritten my Instagram bio more times than I can count. I jot down words on a cocktail napkin and scribble them out just as quickly, revising my identity in every waking moment.

The world will tell you that this is a weakness. I will tell you that it is a strength. To quote myself from earlier in this book, "I cannot tell you the absolute freedom I have felt from embracing the fact that my existence is a paradox. I am not, and will never be, easily digestible for the masses."

So welcome to *Paradoxical!* This is a safe space for the people who grew up constantly being told they were *too much*. Join me in this podcast where we get real and honest on any and everything. Expect me to go from soul-deep spirituality one episode to how to pack for a backpacking trip the next—magical synchronicity stories, navigating the world as a neurodivergent woman, building relationships, confronting grief. There are no labels and no limits.

An anti-niche podcast might not be easily consumable for a mass market, but I will tell you it is *infinitely* more interesting. If you're done with labels, you'll find your people here.

—heather ♥

Scan the QR code below or go to **www.athenarosealchemy.com/the-paradoxical-podcast** to join the paradox :)

Acknowledgements

To Mom. I did it. I finally did it. I hope you are smiling down on me in heaven. When I dance, when I fly, when I sing, it is your spirit moving through me. Thank you for showing me the way forward and instilling in me the courage to follow that guidance. It is a lonely path, but I am never truly alone with you watching over me.

To past Heather. The farther I fall down this rabbit hole, the more I'm in awe of just how brave you were in the beginning there, putting yourself out into the world with unbridled faith and relentless optimism, despite being given so many reasons to become hard and cold. You might be braver than I am. I'm so proud of you for believing in yourself and continuing to build a path toward your dreams, even when the light grew dark and fear clouded every single step. These pages wouldn't exist without you. I wouldn't exist without you. Thank you for seeing the future that I could exist in, and creating a world where I could be born.

To present Heather. Let yourself cry today. The one thing you've always wanted now exists. You are a published author.

To future Heather. Thank you for being my guardian angel. L'eterno ritorno.

To my sisters, Jenny and Nancy. Thank you for watching over me in the years since Mom has passed. And thank you for stepping back and allowing me to learn, to fail, to forge my own path. I'm grateful to know that I still have your love and support, even if you don't fully understand the life that I now live. And thank you, Nancy, for your help in proofreading this book. Your offer to help in the realization of this dream of mine meant the world.

To Jack. We wouldn't have met if not for this book! And you thinking to yourself, *What the heck is this girl doing on a laptop in a noisy hostel on a Saturday night.* Your support helped me to keep going and finally get this book into people's hands. I'm so thankful to have you in my life. You have taught me so much, and it's been beautiful to see the ways in which we've both grown through our friendship.

To Orian. I met you after this book was already written, but now I can't imagine you not being in my life. I'm so grateful for your support during the publishing process. You always see my highest potential and help to point me toward it. I love you so much. I am counting down the days until we are together again.

To Megan. I'm so grateful the universe brought us back together. You were the first person I told about my book. Thank you for your unending support at a time where I continuously doubted myself. Thank you for giving me confidence and helping me to step deeper into my identity as an author. If you hadn't cheered me on, I don't think anyone would be reading this right now.

To Mili. I didn't expect to meet more of my soul family in Italy! I'll never forget those few weeks, just like you'll likely never forget witnessing my horrible attempt at cutting a pizza. Thank you for providing me a safe haven to continue working on this book. And thank you for the amazing podcast cover!

To Morgan. You are forever the first member of my soul family. Words can't describe how much our friendship meant to me at a time when I had almost nothing else. I don't think I need to find the words. I think we both know.

To Alex. Without your help pushing me forward I may have never finished getting all my stuff out of that apartment. You always listened to my aspirations with faith in me rather than skepticism. I keep thinking back to that day we sat in Social Thai Kitchen as I told you my far-off dreams of visiting Thailand, a country that I have now lived in and feels like home. Thank you for believing in me. I hope we really do meet there one day.

To Zulema. Lifetimes have passed since that day on set, and I can still count on you being my number one supporter. Thank you for seeing me. One day I will come back to California so we can skate down the boardwalk in purple rollerblades.

To Jamuna, Carrisa, Chassie, Jillian, Gracie, and Chaney. Thank you for giving me a safe space to heal. Thank you for showing me what being in a space of supportive and empowering women looks like. And thank you, Chassie for delivering a message that I will never forget.

To Chino. I wrote it down! Thank you for showing me the power of patience and persistence. I hope this book ends up in your hands one day.

To my editor, Laura. Working with an editor, handing off my work to be seen by someone else's eyes for the first time, was absolutely terrifying and vulnerable. I'm so grateful to have found you to support me in this process. You encouraged me to believe in myself, pushed me to become a better writer, and helped me make this story the best it can be. Until the next manuscript!

To Divyam. When I sent you those first three chapters, you became the very first person to lay eyes on any part of this book. Sharing it was incredibly terrifying, and your encouragement helped me to continue moving forward. Thank you for your help in proofreading this book, and in showing me the power that this book has. The synchronicities aligned with your reading experience alone, have proved to me that this book is meant to exist in the world.

To Aunt Kathy. Thank you so much for your help in proofreading this book. Since Mom can't be here, it means a lot to have one of her sisters involved.

To my cover artist, Tania. It's not always easy working with someone who has a very clear artistic vision for their book cover! Thank you so much for your dedication and patience while working together. I'm so grateful that you were able to take this idea I had in my mind and bring it to life for the readers.

To my right-hand book man, Phil at Redbrush. Your support in the formatting and publishing stage was invaluable, not only providing clarity whenever needed, but genuine care and understanding. I really don't think this process would have been the same without you, and I'm so thankful you just so happened to find me on Instagram. The universe is always working its magic! Thank you for holding my hand during the painful last steps of publishing, and for not murdering me every time I sent over another extensive edit list for your designer. We may have broken some sort of record for most email threads created on a single project, but I think it was worth it!

To my book coach, Jake. Thank you for your encouragement and positivity as I struggled with deep imposter syndrome. Without you this book likely would have stayed swirling around in my head, rather than sitting on these pages. Thank you for your help in actualizing my dream.

To my photographer, Gabor. Thank you so much for creating a safe space for me to be myself in front of the camera. I am so used to being behind it! Your passion calmed my nerves and it was such a lovely experience co-creating together.

To all my online community. Your kind words have uplifted me on days when I doubt myself, and seeing the impact I have had on your own journeys has continuously inspired me to keep spreading light. I would not be where I am today without all of you, and I am so incredibly grateful.

To the readers. Thank you so much for taking the time to read about my journey, and thank you for your trust. It is my hope that this book has sparked something within you to help aid you on your own path. There is magic and medicine woven into the stories you read.

About the Author

Burnt-out and at her breaking point as a photojournalist, Heather embarked on a self-discovery journey that uprooted her old belief system and led her to share her story on social media. Garnering millions of views and growing a community of over eighty thousand people, Heather is now a spiritual and authenticity mentor that guides people home to their true selves. Her focus is on helping people break the self-created limits that block them from living the lives they want. She also inspires and empowers neurodivergent spiritual women to embrace all parts of themselves in a world that constantly seeks to diminish them. Always leading by example, Heather is constantly seeking out new and challenging experiences and going where the universe guides her, no matter how scary it may seem. Heather has now been traveling around the world with her emerald backpack for over a year since the conclusion of this book, and she has a million more stories and lessons to share! She has also recently embraced the shift from @awakeningheather to @athenarosealchemy on Instagram, representing the ever-evolving nature of her identity. Follow her journey on Instagram at @athenarosealchemy or visit **www.athenarosealchemy.com** for more insights and updates.